EARN MONEY

READING

BOOKS

A FREELANCER'S GUIDE TO THE

PUBLISHING INDUSTRY

BY

ROBERT HANCOCK

&

ELIZABETH ASHTON

FOURTH EDITION © 1992 BROUGHTON HALL INC.

ISBN 0-934748-31-4

Manufactured in the United States of America

PUBLISHER'S NOTE

We have done our best to carefully research and compile this Directory only from sources believed to be authentic and reliable; however, we cannot guarantee total accuracy or completeness.

If you would be kind enough to bring to our attention any errors you may find, we will include your corrections in our next edition. We will also send you a complimentary copy of one of our other reports as a token of our appreciation.

Please note we are not affiliated with any of the companies listed in this publication. Our sole purpose is to provide you with a fund of useful information.

Best of Luck.

THE PUBLISHERS

TABLE OF CONTENTS

Page

1.0 READING — AND MORE 1

  1.1 Publishing is Big Business 1
  Publishing is Very Personal; Spotting a Winner

  1.2 Where Do You Come In? 6
  *"I Don't Know Anything About It"; "I Don't Have The
  Education"; "I Don't Have the Self-confidence"; Three
  Guidelines for Self-starters*

2.0 HOW BOOKS ARE MADE 11

  2.1 The Idea 12
  Non-Fiction Ideas; Fiction Ideas; Stealing Ideas; Ghosting

  2.2 Selling The Idea 15
  *"Flavor of the Month"; "Over the Transom" and Literary
  Agents; Scouts; Timescales; Advances; Outright Sale; Why
  Am I Telling You All This?*

  2.3 The Role of the Publisher's Reader — So Far 20
  *The "Layer" System of Readers; "Flavor of the Month"
  Editing*

  2.4 Danger — Writer At Work 22

  2.5 Editing, Design and Production 22

  2.6 Marketing and Reviewing 22

3.0 THE UNWRITTEN WORD 23

  3.1 Plays 23
  *Performance Before Publication; Publication Before
  Performance*

  3.2 Movie Scripts 25
  *The "Movie of the Book"; Sequels; Treatments; Completed
  Scripts*

  3.3 Tape-Recorded Books 26

  3.4 And Now The Good News 27

4.0 READING FICTION 29

    4.1 Manuscript Mechanics 29
    Typed; Double-Spaced; Adequate Margins; Standard Paper,
    One Side Only; Sequentially Numbered; Other Requirements;
    Authors' Tricks; Your Repressibilities

    4.2 Story... 33
    The "Ten Standard Plots"; Story and Style; Beware of the
    Message

    4.3 Style 36
    Make Comparisons; Try to Set a Date; Spot the Joins

    4.4 Characterization 38
    "Stock" Characters; Characterization Techniques

    4.5 Continuity 40

    4.6 Technique 41
    Spelling; The Great Thesaurus Swindle; Grammar; Style
    Manuals; The Role of the Editor

    4.7 Don't Panic 45

    4.8 Sample Fiction Review 46

5.0 CHILDREN'S FICTION 49

    5.1 Age Considerations 49
    Controlled Vocabularies; Books for Young Children; Books
    for Pre-Teens; Books for Older Children

    5.2 Story 55
    Messages

    5.3 Style 56

    5.4 Characterization 57

    5.5 Continuity 57

    5.6 Technique 58

6.0 PLAYS AND SCREENPLAYS 61

    6.1 Story 61

6.2   Style 62

6.3   Characterization 62

6.4   Continuity 63

6.5   Technique 63

6.6   Stageworthiness 64

7.0   **NON-FICTION** 65

7.1   Experts and Non-Experts 65
*What the Subject-Matter Expert Does; What the General
Reader Does;*

7.2   Content 67
*High-Grade and Low-Grade Facts; Completeness and
Conciseness*

7.3   Structure 70
*Chronological Structures; Thematic Structures; Structures for
Special Applications; Mixed Structures*

7.4   Readability 74
Two Kinds of Dullness

7.5   Technique 75

7.6   Children's Non-Fiction 76

7.7   Sample Non-Fiction Report 77

8.0   **OPPORTUNITIES AT THE WRITING STAGE** 79

8.1   Artwork and Illustration 79
*Tables and Charts; Line Drawings; Spot Color; Half-Tones
and Photographs; Full Color; Copying and "Lifting" Pictures*

8.2   Research 85
Factual Research; Picture Research

8.3   Computer Consultancy 86

8.4   Why Not Write a Book 86
*Write a Proposal/Outline; Write Some Sample Text; Write to
Publishers; Work Like a Dog and Earn Very Little Money*

9.0   OPPORTUNITIES AT THE EDITING STAGE 89
*You Reap the Rewards; This is Where the Opportunities Are; The
Ultimate in Flexibility; Time Is Of The Essence*

    9.1   Copyediting 91
    *Unresolved Questions; Lack of Clarity; Inconsistencies;
    Spelling; Grammar; Punctuation; "House Style"; Copyediting
    on Disk; Another Electronic Swindle*

    9.2   Proofreading 98
    Setting "Off the Disk"; Proofreaders' Marks

    9.3   Indexing 103
    Choosing the Index Entries; Making the Index

    9.4   "Blurb" Writing 104

10.0   MARKETING AND REVIEWING 107

    10.1   Book Marketing 107
    *Press Kits; Press Mailings; Launch Parties; Author Tours;
    Book Reviewing; Content; Quality of Content; Author;
    Competing Books; Publication Data; Other Information*

    10.2   Review Clipping 113

11.0   ACQUIRING AND HONING SKILLS 115

    11.1   Practice 116
    *Book Analysis; Book Reviews; "Blurb" Writing; Writing Press
    Releases; Copyediting; Proofreading; Indexing; Illustration;
    Research; The Parish Magazine and the Community Theater*

    11.2   Books 122

    11.3   Courses 122
    Selecting Courses

12.0   MARKETING YOURSELF 125
*Don't Tell Anyone About This Book; Check Literary Market Place;
Writer's Market*

    12.1   The Freelance Life 127
    Don't Burn Your Bridges; The Good News

    12.2   Start Out Small 129
    Working for Nothing; Expanding Your Base

    12.3   Working With Writers 131

Writers' Groups; Writers' Conferences

12.4   Working as an Agent's or Publisher's Reader   133
Query Letter; Resume

12.5   Working as a "Scout"   135
Query Letter; Don't Overdo It

12.6   Editorial Services   138
Don't Overdo It (Part II); Start Locally

12.7   Publicity   140
The Local Theater Again

12.8   Book Reviews...   141
Syndicate

ENVOI...AND GET PAID FOR IT   144

GLOSSARY AND REFERENCE   145

APPENDICES

Appendix 1: Partial Listing of Children's and Young Adult
             Book Publishers   157
Appendix 2: Partial Listing of Publishers of Books on Tape   163
Appendix 3: Some Canadian Publishing Houses   169
Appendix 4: Employment Agencies   179
Appendix 5: Partial Listing of Some Schools and Courses   181
Appendix 6: Partial Listing of Some Publishers by State   189
Appendix 7: Writing a Reader's Report   203
Appendix 8: Writer's Workshops, Conferences and Classes   205

1.0   READING — AND MORE

It sounds too good to be true, a reader's dream. Read books — and get paid for it? Yes! Believe it or not, it *is* possible. What's more, the fact that you have taken the trouble to send for this Broughton Hall guide is a strong indication that you have the initiative and the ability to get into reading books for profit as well as for fun!

In fact, it is even better than that. As you learn more and more about publishing, you will find that reading — being a "publisher's reader" — is only *one* of the book-related jobs that you can do at home. Effectively, you have just bought two books for the price of one, because you will also learn how you can expand into many other areas of book production — if you want to, that is. You could even end up as a writer, for that matter: it is sad, but true, that many writers fail not because they do not know how to write, but because they do not know how the publishing business works. When you have finished this book, you will know how publishing works; and when you have gained some experience, you may even find yourself lecturing at writers' conferences to the very people whose work will one day come through your mailbox.

1.1   PUBLISHING IS BIG BUSINESS

The simple truth is that publishing is big business. Although it is fashionable to complain about the decline of reading, the fact is that more books are being published than ever before — and more people are reading them. The decline is relative, to be sure: many people don't read, preferring instead to watch football on TV or to play video games. But the population of the United States is more than two hundred and fifty *million* people; and most of the ones who read books are going to be reading them in English. This translates into an absolutely enormous market, far bigger than in Europe where English is only one of the languages in use. Of course, if you are fluent in another language, you may find work reading (or editing, or whatever) in that language, where there may be hardly anyone else available who knows the publishing business *and* speaks the language fluently.

It also translates into a market where many millions of dollars change hands all the time, from the reader who pays a few bucks for the latest book by his (or her) favorite author, to the media magnate who spends hundreds of millions on acquiring another publishing house. With that much money around, you would think that there must be some way of making some of it stick to your fingers. You would be right. There are several, and this book tells you about almost all of them — about all of the ones you can do as a freelance, that is, as distinct from how to buy a publishing house or a printing works! The sheer *size* of the publishing business is one of the keys to why there is a constant demand for freelances.

Publishing is Very Personal

Although publishing is a very big business, it is also a very personal business. Many successful publishing houses have been founded by just one person with a "nose" for good books: someone who can spot, almost infallibly, what is going to sell. Then, success brings growth; and after a while, the chances are that one of the senior commissioning editors will grow tired of working for a big, bureaucratic organization, so they will leave and set up their own publishing house. Then, the whole process begins over again.

Ultimately, though, the most important person is the reader — that's you and me — and there's no doubt that our preferences are very personal indeed: each of us is likely to have favorite authors that the other has never heard of, and there may be whole categories of books that we can't agree on. You may read romances, while I read science fiction and the person over there reads Westerns; and none of us would pay a penny for the others' books.

This is another of the keys to why there are so many opportunities for freelances in the publishing business. Books are not like cheese, to be sold by the pound. You can't mass-produce books. You can mass-produce a single title, and that is the aim of every publisher in the world, because it's what we call a best-seller; but then there's another title along, and it has to be treated completely differently, so we are back to square one. Because it is almost impossible for one person to be equally at home with every different kind of book, publishing is *always* very fragmented, and publishers need all the help they can get!

Spotting a Winner

This big, fragmented, personal business is further complicated by the fact that there is no sure and certain formula for picking a best-seller. Even "big-name" writers have been known to write some truly awful books, and a big name is one of the best guarantees a publisher can get that a book will sell; but it won't work every time.

Publishers know, therefore, that they are likely to have three kinds of books on their lists. About ten percent of the titles they publish will account for ninety percent of their profits; another forty or fifty percent will make a modest profit; and the rest will, if they are lucky, break even — though a significant percentage of these will actually make a loss.

Why, then, do they take these risks? Why does *any* publisher put out books that make a loss? There are three reasons. The first is that publishing is a gamble. The second is that one of the things that keeps the book trade alive is the willingness of most publishers to make that gamble. The third is that if they want to maintain credibility as publishers, they *have* to publish a good mixture of books.

Publishing is a Gamble — As I have already said, there are no sure and certain formulas for predicting a winner. There are countless stories of books which publishers thought would make a modest profit, but which instead turned into runaway best-sellers, or flopped completely. All they can do is to give it their best guess.

Taking the Risk — You might think that it would be possible for a publisher to buy *only* books from proven best-selling authors. In fact they can't. If they did, they would soon find that they were being challenged by another publishing house, with an author no-one had heard of, but who turned out to be at least as good as the established best-seller. After all, even the money-making megastars like Stephen

King had to start somewhere! Also, as I have already said, "best-selling" authors can and do write books that do not sell, and if they were not acutely aware that they faced serious competition from other writers, there are at least some of them who would grow lazy and churn out "formula" stories. To top it all, established authors can command big advances, and they may be tempted away by a better offer from another publisher, so publishing only "big names" is a very expensive course to take. Obviously, such a policy could easily lead to a decline in sales and a decline for any publishing house that did not have a good mix of both new and established authors.

Credibility — Finally, publishing is not quite the same sort of business as others. A publisher who treats his authors as raw material, and his editorial and production staff like factory hands, will soon find that very few people want to do business with him. A publisher has to look as if he is genuinely interested in what he is doing, or the *intelligentsia* — the people who help to form public opinion through the media — will soon start to make snide remarks about him, subtly poisoning his name through the business. Some publishers will even publish books that they *know* are going to be flops, but which they think are sufficiently interesting to be worth publishing, either because they genuinely care about the book or because they want to look as if they do.

Once again, this means that there are plenty of opportunities for freelances of all kinds. In particular, it relates to the title of this book, *EARN MONEY READING BOOKS*. Because publishers cannot judge *all* tastes, they rely on other people to help them. One of those "other people" could easily be *you*. Publishers need people who can give an opinion on children's stories, or on nuclear physics; on romances, or on detailed histories; on science fiction, or on home-repair manuals. The chances are that you could not give an informed opinion on all of those, but you could probably comment meaningfully on at least one of them; and even if you couldn't, there are countless other subjects where your opinion *would* be valuable, whether it is on Westerns or philosophy, handguns or crocheting, art or computers.

The Publishers — Many media magnates, who have made their money in television or in newspapers, try to buy respectability by buying old-established publishing houses. Ask yourself, though, what they are buying. If they really wanted to be publishers, they could set up a new publishing house from scratch. What they really want is the *image* of being a publisher: a patron of the arts, hobnobbing with literary figures and the intelligentsia. If they are nice people, the intelligentsia will drink their champagne and accept them into the fold. If they are not, the name of the publishing house will go through the floor, and all the staff will leave; and all the magnate will have for his money is the "back list" (the books already published) and egg on his face.

One result of this "bought" prestige, though, is that many publishing magnates know little or nothing about book publishing. They therefore have to rely on their staff, who in turn will rely on freelance help — and once again, this could mean *you*.

The People who Work in Publishing — To this day, there is a certain glamour associated with working in publishing; as I say, it's not like being in the cheese trade, or a dealer in used motor vehicles.

This glamorous image, whether it is justified or not, forces down the salaries that are paid in the lower echelons of publishing — there are always people who are willing to work for next to nothing, just to be in publishing rather than in (say) a factory or a bank — which in turn means that there is quite a high turnover of salaried staff. A high turnover means that publishers are forever training new staff, and that there is often quite poor continuity of staff. A reliable freelance, therefore, is all the more highly prized because he or she (a) knows the business and (b) provides continuity. Needless to say, this "reliable freelance" could be you!

Don't forget, too, that the prestige of publishing rubs off on you:

"What are you doing now?"

"Oh, I'm a publisher's reader," (or an indexer, or a copyeditor, or a proofreader, or any one of a dozen other jobs).

Sounds good, doesn't it?

1.2   <u>WHERE DO YOU COME IN?</u>

You probably sent for this book because you read a lot, and you thought it would be a wonderful idea to turn your hobby into income. Now, even if you read more than anyone else you know, and even if you are one of the many people who (quite rightly) deplore the decline in the popularity of reading, you have to admit that you can't be the only voracious reader in the United States. Doesn't this mean, then, that you are facing ferocious competition if you start looking for freelance work in publishing?

Quite honestly, no. There are plenty of reasons why most people don't apply for freelance work, and this is the place to look at them.

<u>"I Don't Know Anything About It"</u>

True enough: most people don't. But once you have read this book, you *will* know enough about it. I know this book wasn't cheap; I know what it's like to *need* (as distinct from merely *wanting*) extra money. That is why I have tried to make this book as informative as possible.

<u>"I Don't Have the Education"</u>

Well, maybe. The fascinating thing is, though, that even if you *really don't* have much of an education, and if you can't tell a verb from a noun, you can *still* read books and get paid for it!

Admittedly, you will have to write reports on the books you read, and the reports will have to be legible, but if you have the knack of spotting a potential best-seller, the publisher won't care if you left school when you were twelve. Remember, the term is best-*seller*, and almost by definition, the majority of people who buy best-sellers are not college professors or professional writers. If you are "Mrs. Average," you may be just the person to spot a big new talent in romance writing, or in children's stories; and if you are "Mr. Average," you may be the person they want to spot next year's best-selling adventure story.

Also, if you want to, you can acquire more skills — there's more about that in Section 4 of this book — but think about this for a minute; you already read a fair amount, and so you *already* know a good deal about the subject. You may not have much practice at putting your reactions into words, but this book is designed to help you do this, too!

"I Don't Have the Self-confidence"

This is The Big One. You can phrase it a hundred different ways: you can call it self-confidence, or credibility, or you can just have that uncomfortable feeling inside yourself that you're not good enough to do the job.

What it comes down to, though, is this: You don't believe in yourself, and therefore you don't expect other people to believe in you. You're putting yourself down.

Now, I don't know you personally. But I do know that you have the energy and initiative to send for this book. I also know that it will take more energy, and more initiative, to offer your services to publishers as a reader. If you can handle the first part — ordering this book — there is no reason why you should not also be able to handle the second part, writing to publishers to offer your services as a freelance. In fact, it should be *easier* to write to the publishers, because you've got a much stronger incentive: instead of *you* paying *us* for a book, *they* are going to pay *you*. And instead of buying a book on a subject about which you knew very little, you are offering a service about which you know a great deal — or at least, about which you will know a great deal when you have finished this book!

I am not saying that the first letter you write to a publisher will bring in lucrative contracts (though it might). I am not even saying that the tenth letter will bring in lucrative contracts — though if you have not had a favorable response by then, you might want to re-read Chapter 12, MARKETING YOURSELF, in order to refine your selling letter. But even if you write fifty letters (and I sincerely doubt that you will write that many), you will still have spent well under $20 on postage and stationary and you could well land work that earns you literally thousands of dollars. Almost certainly, you will find that *somewhere* out there, there is a publisher who is interested in you.

Three Guidelines for Self-starters

In modern business life, everyone has to be a "self-starter." This means that you can't just wait for someone to tell you what to do: you have to take the initiative. This requires self confidence — self confidence you may not think you have.

Well, no-one is 100 percent self-confident 100 percent of the time. I have interviewed millionaires and the heads of successful businesses, and even they are not totally self-confident the whole time. If you feel your self-confidence flagging (and it's something that happens to all of us sometimes), remember three things:

The first is that you are almost certainly better educated and better qualified than you think. Look at the people around you. You probably know plenty of people who hardly read anything at all. They can't do the jobs described in this book. You can.

The second is that if you don't play, you can't win. If you are too shy and modest to write to publishers, they are never going to know that you exist. If you do write to them, on the other hand, the worst that will happen is that they send you a polite rejection slip — a bit depressing, and a small blow to the self-confidence, but easily forgotten. The best that can happen is that you land a big contract.

The third is that once you have finished this book, you will have access to a whole armory of knowledge that many other people simply do not have. Before you start, you're ahead. If there are setbacks along the way — well, that's life, isn't it? It won't all be setbacks, though; and from experience, I can tell you that a single $5000 contract can offset an awful lot of setbacks!

2.0   HOW BOOKS ARE MADE

Most people have no idea of the process by which a book is published — or if they do, their ideas are often romantic, inaccurate, and outdated. They imagine an author struggling in a garret, laboring to produce a masterpiece; the publishers, foolishly rejecting the book time and again; the final breakthrough, when some editor recognizes genius; a best seller; and lots of money all round.

Well, yes. Sometimes — very rarely — it does happen that way. But to be honest, few authors are geniuses; few books are masterpieces; and very few masterpieces are best-sellers which earn large sums of money. From all this, it follows that publishing does not really work in the way that the romantics imagine. With non-fiction, the gap between the romantic dream and the real world is enormous.

Later in this book, I'll come back to the different ways in which fiction and non-fiction are judged, but for now, it is enough to say this:

If you want to be a writer, write non-fiction. You are unlikely ever to get rich, but at least you have a good chance of earning a living — assuming, of course, that you are reasonably competent. Writing fiction is *much* more of a lottery. You need to be very, very good to earn anything at all; and at any one time, there are probably only a couple of dozen fiction writers *at most* who are in the "superstar" bracket, with automatic sales of more than 100,000 for almost anything they write. The vast majority of fiction writers (and a smaller majority of non-fiction writers, for that matter) have to have other jobs in order to support their writing habit. I even knew one who worked as an IRS auditor on Mondays, Wednesdays and Fridays, so that he could work as a writer the rest of the week.

Now, you may not want to be a writer, in which case you may have skipped the last paragraph on the grounds that it did not apply to you. If you did skip it, go back and read it. It tells you a lot about the publishing process. Non-fiction is the staple of many publishers, and many writers: we live in the "information age," and non-fiction books are still the mainstay of the information business. Fiction is a smaller, chancier market, *but* the rewards for the right book can be immense.

All right: how *does* the book business really work?

2.1 THE IDEA

Today, it is comparatively rare for a book to be finished before it is sold. Instead of a complete manuscript, the author sells two things: an idea, and his (or her) track record.

Non-fiction Ideas

Clearly, it is easier to sell a non-fiction book on this basis than it is to sell a fiction book. The fiction author can give the publisher a chapter-by-chapter analysis of the book, and the publisher can see from this whether there is likely to be a market for this particular book. Then, depending on the author's track record (the number of books he or she has had published), the publisher may ask for a greater or lesser amount of sample text. If the sample text looks good, and the idea looks good, the publisher will offer the writer a contract.

Sometimes, the idea comes from the publisher, rather than from the author. The publisher will approach a writer with a good track record in a particular field, and will ask if he or she is interested in writing a book on a particular subject. They will kick the idea around for a while; the writer will normally produce the same kind of outline as already described; and once again, a contract will be signed.

In general, the only time that publishers will employ readers at the "ideas" stage is when they are not sure about sample text. In other words, they have already accepted the idea: what they want to learn more about is execution.

At one company where I used to work, we used to produce self-instructional "how-to" material. In order to make sure that this "how-to" material really was understandable, we had to try it out on people.

The standard test, before the company would hire anyone, was to have them write a brief self-instructional piece on how to build brick walls, using the different patterns that bricklayers call "bonding." The would-be employee had to explain the different types of bonding clearly and concisely, in a self-instructional format, and then the office junior or someone else would be given the instructional material and a box of children's toy bricks, and asked to build a particular type of wall using a particular type of bonding. If they succeeded, the applicant was accepted. If they failed, the applicant might either be rejected, or given a second chance.

Now, as you probably know, the ways in which people can misunderstand things are countless, so we had to find people who were not very clever, and try the ideas out on them. Of course, we had to conceal the fact that we chose them because they were not very clever, but this little story certainly makes it clear that there is a place even for the least educated freelance in the publishing business!

Actually, you do not need to be unintelligent to be a good test subject for this kind of exercise. It is enough to be "all thumbs." If you are more at home in the world of ideas and of books, but not too good at practical matters, you might be an ideal person to test out illustrated "how to" books. Heaven knows, there are plenty of college professors who could not bake a cake or tune an automobile carburetor!

Fiction Ideas

Normally, a fiction writer's first book — even his or her first two or three books — will be written speculatively; that is, they will have been completed before they are sold. After that, the author may be able to sell the next book on the basis of an outline and a few pages of sample text.

The easiest fiction to sell is the sort of fiction that has an established story-line and established characters. These books are the equivalent of soap-operas: people get hooked on a particular series, and will buy any books in that series, almost regardless of quality. Sometimes, a single series will be supported by a number of writers. For example, the well-known *Conan the Barbarian* series contains books by several different authors.

The next easiest type of fiction to sell is "genre" fiction. "Genre" fiction (or "category" fiction) are the terms that publishers use for romances, historical fiction, science fiction, murder/detective mysteries, Westerns, horror, war stories and so forth. People who read "genre" fiction know that some books are better than others, but they are resigned to the fact that much of the stuff they read will be of fairly low quality. The "genre" that I like most is science fiction, and I have read some appalling trash — but every now and then, I find something really good. You probably feel the same about your favorite type of fiction.

The most difficult type of fiction to sell is the original novel that deals with real people in the real world. A really good fiction writer can make his reader *care* about his characters' emotions and reactions and suffering — which is a pretty good trick when you think about it, because why should anyone care about what happens to a made-up character?

No matter what kind of fiction you are talking about, readers are rarely involved at the "ideas" stage. Normally, they will only become involved at the buying stage (Section 2.2, below), or the editing and production stage (Section 2.4). Even so, it is important for anyone in the publishing business to understand how each stage works.

Stealing Ideas

People who have never been involved in the publishing business are always worried about ideas being "stolen" by unscrupulous publishers. In fact, this almost never happens. There are three good reasons why publishers normally do not steal ideas.

In the first place, ideas are ten a penny. Everybody and his dog has at least one idea for a book, and frequently, a publisher is offered two or three similar ideas at the same time. Sometimes, the authors who are unsuccessful will complain that their ideas are "stolen," but in truth, it is more likely that their ideas (or more likely, their presentation and writing skills) were inferior to another writer's.

In the second place, *someone* has to write the book. If a publisher decides to buy an idea, he will usually get a better book from the author who thought of the idea than he would get if he brought someone else in: most writers hate working to someone else's plan. If the idea really is good, but the writer is totally incompetent, the publisher might ask another writer if he or she is interested in a book on a similar topic, but this is as close as you normally get to "stealing," unless you count "ghosting," which is described below.

In the third place, "stolen" books rarely sell well — largely because of the reasons given in the last paragraph. They normally are not very good, and that is all there is to it.

Ghosting

"Ghosting" or "ghost writing" is where someone has a story to tell, but lacks the skill to write it down. A skilled professional writer is then brought in to act as a "ghost writer." As the name suggests, the "ghost" usually writes as if he or she were the person whose story it is.

2.2   SELLING THE IDEA

In the last section, I glossed over the way in which the idea is actually bought and sold. The truth is that the whole process is very complex. The author's original idea is frequently modified by the publisher. For example, it may be more heavily illustrated, or less heavily illustrated. It may have its "slant" changed: for example, one travel book publisher may want to include "hard" hotel and restaurant data, while another travel book publisher may prefer to stick to "atmospheric" writing, because hotel information soon goes out of date. With fiction, particularly with movie scripts, it is by no means unusual for characters to change their identity, their race, their nationality or even their sex.

As I have already said, fiction writers often have to complete their first book (or two or three books, or more) before they can try to sell them; and as a publisher's reader, this is likely to be the form in which you first encounter fiction.

"Flavor of the Month"

Taken to extremes, excessive editorial and marketing input becomes what writers disparagingly call "flavor of the month" rewrites. Feminists are big? Great; we'll make the central character a feminist. Native Americans? Can't we make the hero a Native American? Everyone is concerned about the disabled? Let's do a book called "Do-It-Yourself Projects for the Disabled." If you think that the last crack is in bad taste, you ought to hear some of the editors I have talked to in the past!

On the other hand, you do have to remember that in the final analysis, publishing depends on selling a large number of books, so marketing considerations cannot be ignored completely. If the marketing "slant" is too obvious in the book, it will be a failure; but the author who completely ignores popular appeal must do so at his own risk!

"Over the Transom" and Literary Agents

Basically, publishers buy books from one of three sources. One is "over the transom," the common publishers' term for the vast quantity of unsolicited material that they receive all the time. The second is via literary agents, and the third is directly from authors with whom they already have an established relationship.

"Over the transom" submissions are traditionally regarded with dread by publishers, but their dread is two -edged. The vast majority of "over-the-transom" material is unspeakably bad; but they dare not simply return it (or throw it away) without reading it, because there is always the chance that somewhere in the "slush pile" (the stack of unsolicited manuscripts) there is *something* that could earn them a million dollars. Clearly, this is one of the major openings for the publisher's reader — a topic I shall come back to in Section 2.3.

For most publishers, though, their "bread and butter" comes from submissions via agents. Typically, writers find that getting an agent is a "Catch-22" situation: you can't sell books without an agent, and you can't get an agent unless you have already had some books published.

Fortunately for you, though, some agents are willing to take on the publishers' "slush piles." The reason they do it is obvious: they are hoping to find the next million-selling popular novelist, so that they can take their fifteen percent (most modern agents take fifteen percent, though some of the older-established ones still work on ten percent. What the agents do, though, is charge the authors "reading fees" of $50, $100 or more. They don't make money on this, but they just about cover their expenses: and if they do discover a good book, they make the agent's fee! As you can see, they also have to employ readers; and that is why many "publisher's readers" today are actually *agents'* readers.

Finally, there are the books that publishers buy directly from authors that they already know. Independent readers almost never see these, because the author and the publisher already have a very good understanding, and there is no need for external vetting. It is however conceivable (though far from common) that an author or even a publisher might be willing to pay a reader to vet such a book, especially if there is specialist knowledge involved. For example, an author might have written a book on (say) Ford Mustang cars, and it would be worth a couple of hundred dollars to him to have the text checked by an expert on the subject.

Scouts

There is also an interesting "in-between" way in which books are bought. Some publishers retain "scouts," people who look out for good writers who are not nationally known. They may be published locally, or they may appear in highly specialized or limited-circulation publications. They may even be unknowns, meeting at writers' circles or giving their material out to friends.

The scout's job is to watch out for undiscovered talent, and to notify the publisher when he finds it. Note that he or she does *not* approach the writer; that is left for the publisher to do. If the publisher signs a contract with the writer as a result of the scout's introduction, the scout receives a "finder's fee." There is more about scouting — a surprisingly little-known field, but with many opportunities for the person with wide-ranging interests and (preferably) a good range of contacts — in Section 12.5.

Timescales

Many people are shocked when they learn how long it takes to produce a book. Typically, an idea may be hawked around for a year or more by an author or his agent before it sells; and from the first "bite" to the signing of the contracts can easily take three or four months. Then, if the book is not already written, the author will have anything from six months to a couple of years in which to write it. After delivery, the editorial process normally takes a minimum of three months, but again it can stretch to years; and then printing and production takes another three months or so.

The bottom line is that a book normally takes a minimum of a year from signature of contract to publication; two years is not unusual; and a really bad publisher (and there are plenty of them around!) can take five years or more, even if the author delivers on time.

At the other extreme, it is possible for a book to be written in a month or less; edited and designed in another month to six weeks; and then published two or three months after that. In fact, I knew one publisher who did a very successful book on the wedding of Prince of Wales and Lady Diana Spencer. Most of the book — the historical and personal material — was already written and designed by the day of the wedding, but space was left to "drop in" the actual wedding pictures and an appropriate amount of text. The editor flew out to the printer with the pictures and the text, and the book was in the shops a week later.

Advances

Many people are also shocked when they realize how small authors' advances often are. Because the general public normally only hears about the six-figure "glamour" advances, they imagine that all writers are given handsome advances for all books. This is a long way from the truth.

In fact, some publishers do not pay advances *at all*: the author does not see a penny until the books start selling. When you consider that a book may involve considerable expenses in travel and illustrations, to say nothing of living expenses while the writer is working on it, you can see that a writer's life can be precarious!

With the better publishers, and with established writers, things are slightly better. Even then, advances are far from princely. Many writers have never seen a $10,000 advance — and although $10,000 may sound like a lot of money, remember that this might be a writer's *only* income for many months, or even for a year or more. Typical advances for non-fiction books are in the $2000 to $10,000 range.

What is more, the advance is never paid "up front," all at once. Typically, the writer receives fifty percent on signature of contract and fifty percent on delivery. Then, when the book starts selling (*if* it starts selling) the advance has to be "earned out" before they get any more money. Typically, an author receives ten percent of the cover price of a hardback book, and eight percent on paperbacks. This means that a $4.95 paperback earns only about forty cents per copy, so you need to sell 25,000 copies in order to earn back a $10,000 advance.

Outright Sale

Some books are not sold on an advance/royalty basis; they are bought outright by the publisher. Typically, the publishers pay anything from about two cents a word to about a quarter a word. A typical short non-fiction book is about 15,000 to 30,000 words, and if commissioned on an outright sale basis will fetch anything from about $2500 upwards.

Why am I Telling You All This?

All this financial information may not seem to be too relevant to being a publisher's reader, but on the other hand, you cannot really understand the publishing business without having some insight into the economics of it. Besides, it is natural human curiosity to want to know what the next guy earns. Quite often, publishers' readers may earn more than the writers whose work they read — and, of course, many writers find that reading other writers' manuscripts is a useful source of income!

If you are a writer, you may also find that a better understanding of other people's work will give you a better understanding of your own work, too.

2.3   THE ROLE OF THE PUBLISHER'S READER — SO FAR!

You will already have seen where the publisher's reader fits in so far — and note that I say "so far," because there is much more to come. At the "ideas" stage, you may be consulted on either style or content; and at the sales stage, especially where a completed manuscript already exists, you really come into your own.

The "Layer" System of Readers

Most publishers and agents who employ readers use a "two-layer" or "multi-filter" system.

Their first line of defense against bad manuscripts (and their first welcome for good ones) is a fast reader who skims through everything and weeds out the completely unreadable stuff. There is always a lot of this. Some of it may be literally illegible, a hand-scribbled scrawl. Some of it may be immaculately presented on a word processor, but completely without originality or interest. As Doctor Johnson once said to a would-be writer, "Your work is both interesting and original; but unfortunately, the interesting parts are not original, and the original part is not interesting."

The first reader (actually, there may be several of them) may be either in-house or freelance. Once the manuscript has got past him or her, it goes on to the next layer, where it may be read by anything up to three or four readers who give a more detailed appraisal. If the first reader spoke very highly of it, the manuscript may be sent to a number of second-layer readers simultaneously; but if, as is more usual, it is just a "maybe," it will be passed from one reader to the next. These "second-layer" readers are almost invariably freelances.

One word of warning here, though. The terminology I have used — "layers" — is by no means standardized; and also, it is quite common for the publisher or agent to perform the work of the person I have called the "first reader," so that as far as they are concerned, the freelances to whom they farm out the work are the "first readers." When you write in, by all means make it clear that you are familiar with the business, but don't start using my terminology as if it were accepted jargon, because it isn't.

Bear in mind that freelance reading is still a very flexible sort of business, and publishers are more likely to be impressed by your general knowledge and aptitude than they are to be impressed with the fact that you have read this book. After all, what this book is about is how to use the information and knowledge *that you already have*: it is a *key* to a career, not the career itself.

"Flavor of The Month" Editing

I discussed earlier the difficulty of steering a path between "flavor of the month," editing (and writing) and material that lacks popular appeal.

As a publisher's reader, it is part of your job to spot both kinds of problems. If the book smacks too much of "flavor of the month," you need to say so; but if in your opinion it could be made more popular by making a few simple changes — cutting out long-winded historical patches, perhaps, or reducing the tendency of the author to "talk down to" his public — then it is your duty to point that out, too.

Also, you need to watch out for out-of-date "flavors of the month." Because of the time scale of book production, a topic that was hot when the book was commissioned may be stone-cold by the time it is delivered.

2.4 DANGER — WRITER AT WORK

There is much more in Chapter 8 about what *you* might be able to contribute at the writing stage, but for the moment, all I need to point out is that writing is by no means as solitary an occupation as you might have thought. *If he or she can afford it*, a writer will use researchers, artists and photographers — and if you have the skills, you can actually be involved at the sharp end, the place where the creative process is actually happening.

2.5 EDITING, DESIGN AND PRODUCTION

Again, this is the subject of another chapter — Chapter 9 — but (as I have already said earlier in the chapter), this is a very time-consuming part of the making of a book. It is also a very important time, because this is when the appearance and general "feel" of the book are established. Often, the difference between a cheap-and-nasty looking book, and a really handsome-looking book, is nothing to do with money: it is the difference between a good designer and a bad designer, a good artist and a bad artist. Likewise, the difference between a clear, crisp, easy-to-use reference work and a book that is hard to follow, sloppy and ill-thought-out is the difference between a good copy editor and a bad copy editor. Even the humble proofreader can make a great difference to a book, and as any professional scholar will tell you, a good index can transform a book from being an "also-ran" of limited usefulness into an indispensable reference work.

2.6 MARKETING AND REVIEWING

As with the previous two sections, Marketing and Reviewing the subject of a whole chapter in its own right, Chapter 10. But there *is* room for freelance book marketers, and there is even more room for freelance book reviewers. These are all jobs that *you* will be able to consider after you have finished this book!

3.0   **THE UNWRITTEN WORD**

Plays; movie scripts; books recorded on cassette tapes ... there are several media where, although the word starts out in written form, the form in which it reaches the "consumer" — the audience — is not written.

The opportunities for the freelances — that's *you* — are not as widespread in these fields as they are in conventional publishing, but they still exist, and that is why there is a brief chapter here that deals with what you may be able to do. In all fairness, it reads more like a chapter of what *not* to do, because the opportunities really are rather limited. This is why it is a brief chapter! On the other hand, if you know where *not* to waste your effort, you will have a much better idea of where you *should* make the effort!

3.1   **PLAYS**

There are two separate paths by which plays may be published. The traditional one is that a play is written for a particular theater company, or at least, it is written and then offered to various theater companies, one of which eventually takes it up. Only after the play has been accepted, and tried out on the stage, will it be published. Sometimes, it is not even written until it has been hammered out on stage, with input from all concerned; this process is known as "workshopping" a play. The other route treats the play more like a novel: it is written, sold to a publisher, published, and then performed. We can call the first route "performance before publication," and the second route "publication before performance."

Performance Before Publication

There are very few opportunities for the true outsider here. You really need to be involved in an existing theater company or theater holding company to find out what is circulating in typescript — and even then, the decision to produce a play is normally taken by a very small group of theater professionals, or possibly just by one person.

About the only way that a freelance can be involved is at the "preview" stage, where the play has been accepted and produced, but the opening is in a small theater instead of a big one: the classic "off-Broadway" production. The "off-Broadway" production is intended as a pilot or test run, to see how the play "works" in front of a live audience. Then, the play may be altered before it is shown at a major venue. Whole scenes may be added or dropped; the emphasis on the characters may be changed; and in extreme cases, the play may be dropped altogether.

Even with "off-Broadway" productions, the play is normally run as a commercial proposition, with a paying audience. It is only at the first few performances — which are more like dress rehearsals — that the audiences are specially invited.

If you live in a city with a strong "live" theater (especially New York), and *if* you are so interested in theater that you can keep in touch with the "theater scene," and *if* the director decides that a "test run" would be a good idea before he goes for a paying audience, there may be the occasional opportunity to see a brand-new play and to have some input on how it might be changed. There will never be any financial reward, but the intangible rewards include the fascination of working with creative people, the chance to see good, new plays for little or nothing, and (if the play is a success) the opportunity to say that you saw it before it was even an "off-Broadway" production.

Publication Before Performance

In this case, the route to publication is (as has already been suggested) more like that for a novel; and much of the information given in Chapter 4, as well as the material in Chapter 6, will be relevant.

It is worth adding, though, that if you are not familiar with script conventions, you are unlikely to be very good at reading play scripts. A script is *much* more tiring to read than a novel, partly because of the layout and partly because a good deal of what will make the final play a success (or a failure) is in the hands of the director. If you are not familiar with the mechanics of scripting, Chapter 6 will tell you more.

3.2   MOVIE SCRIPTS

Unlike plays, which are normally published via one of two routes as described above, movie scripts may come from at least four different sources, as described below.

It is also worth noting that movies are sometimes previewed to selected audiences before the final cut is made (in the confusing language of movie-land, a "cut" refers to the final form of the film, so occasionally a "cut" may result in a longer movie. These previews are normally held in out-of-the-way towns, well away from Los Angeles and New York, to see what "normal" people think of the movie. In general, though, the chances of getting onto a preview "circuit" are even smaller than the chances of seeing a play in preview off-Broadway form. To return to the four sources for movies, they are:

The "Movie of the Book"

In this case, the producer buys the rights to an existing book — often, an existing best-seller. Needless to say, there are no opportunities for the freelance here.

Sequels

A remarkable number of movies are sequels — just think of the endless "Rocky" films, or of "Back to the Future," which, after a witty and original start, has turned into little more than a soap opera in which the episodes are a year apart. Once again, there are no opportunities for the freelance.

Treatments

Traditionally, movies were based on "treatments," and this approach still survives for the few original movies that are made today. A "treatment" is a *very* brief story outline, with a minimum of characterization, that is designed to be read in a few minutes: it may consist of as little as a single page.

Because a "treatment" can be read in a few minutes even by a near-illiterate (who are less common today in Hollywood than they used to be), there is usually no need for a publisher's reader. On the other hand, *some* agents may employ readers to go through the "treatments" in the "slush pile" of unsolicited manuscripts.

Completed Scripts

Finally, *some* agents may employ readers to go through completed scripts which come "over the transom" and are added to the "slush pile." Allegedly, there is a lot of work for movie-script readers, but you have to be a member of the Story Analysts Union in order to do it, and (like most unionized jobs in Hollywood and the arts) it is not easy to get your union "ticket." It is the usual "Catch-22": no ticket until you have paid experience, no paid experience until you have a ticket. The only way in is to tell a studio that you *will* join the union — as soon as they hire you!

There is much more about reading completed scripts in Chapter 6.

3.3   TAPE-RECORDED BOOKS

A few years back, someone had the idea of tape-recording books so that people could play the tapes on their way to work or when they were traveling. Since then, this has been a fast-growing market; you can even get the Bible on tape!

Tape-recorded books have a couple of drawbacks. In the first place, they are normally abridged, because reading a full-length book out loud is very time-consuming. Secondly, *hearing* a book is very different from *reading* it, especially if the reader's accent grates on your ears. An Englishman attempting an American accent, or an American attempting an English accent, is usually quite unsuccessful.

With these drawbacks in mind — and also with the proviso that tape-recorded books are normally selected from successfully published books, so publishers' readers are not required — there are limited opportunities for freelance readers in this field. In this case, though, "reading" means "reading out loud."

Quite honestly, this is a strictly "fringe" activity. The number of people who read books out loud onto tape is tiny, and most of them are actors who are between jobs; a hungry actor (a common breed) can be hired very cheaply. If, however, you have a good speaking voice with a fairly neutral accent, you may consider it worth your while to make five-minute "demo" (demonstration) cassette tapes and to send them out to those companies listed in Appendix 1 who are in the recorded-book business. Don't expect to get the tapes back; record them on the best machine you can get, using good-quality tape (though there is no need to use super-expensive "metal" tape); and send them with a cover letter. Before you make them, listen to some professionally-recorded tapes (many libraries stock recorded books) so that you can see what you are up against. *Don't* make full-length tapes: five minutes is the most that any executive is going to listen to!

3.4 <u>And Now the Good News</u>

You may feel that this chapter has been discouraging. To a large extent, you are right. Then again, I don't feel bad about discouraging you from trying to get involved in risky, small-volume work — because there is steady, reliable, large-volume work available elsewhere in the publishing industry, and in the next chapter, we shall look at one of the steadiest and most reliable opportunities of all.

Even so, there *are* a few opportunities in the area of what I have called "the unwritten word," and even if you are unlikely to make much money, you can have fun; which is another reason why this chapter is included.

4.0 <u>READING FICTION</u>

You could be the very first person to read a best-seller — and you could get paid to do it! After the last chapter, which may have seemed a bit discouraging, this chapter has very little in it apart from good news, and information about how to cash in on the permanent flood of books that are published every year.

As already explained in Chapters One and Two, not all works of fiction are read by publishers' readers or agents' readers. There are, however, two categories which provide enormous opportunities for the freelance. These are, first, the "slush pile" and second, books by new authors where the agent or publisher is not sure about the appeal of the book. This chapter tells you how to read a work of fiction critically. We shall look at the story; at style; at characterization; at continuity; and at technique. Don't be worried if you are not too clear on the meaning of some of these terms: you will understand them much better once you have read this chapter.

Before we go on to these topics, though, there is one other subject which is even more important; the form in which the manuscript arrives.

4.1 <u>MANUSCRIPT MECHANICS</u>

It may seem strange to say that the physical state of the manuscript is more important than anything else, but it is. The reason is simple. A messy manuscript will rarely be read. If it is too hard to read, it will be returned to the author (assuming that postage and packaging were supplied), or simply thrown away.

The basic rules for a good, legible manuscript are simple. It should be typed; double-spaced; with adequate margins; on one side of good-quality standard paper; and sequentially numbered. Although you are unlikely to receive manuscripts which do not meet these requirements, it is worth knowing a little bit more about them, because editors will expect you to be familiar with the "ground rules."

Also, there may be occasions when you do get a hard-to-read manuscript, whether because of a mistake on the part of the publisher or agent, or because the author has paid a reading fee and the manuscript is only slightly sub-standard. In this case, a criticism of the manuscript mechanics may well be as useful to the author as a criticism of his writing: it will certainly help to make sure that his or her next manuscript is more acceptable.

Typed

"Typed" obviously includes "printed from a word processor," but it is worth making the point that dot-matrix printing (the sort where each letter is made up of a number of tiny dots) must be "near letter quality" (NLQ). The sort where you can see the individual dots is very hard and tiring to read, and most agents or publishers will not expect you to read such a manuscript. Laser printers or ink-jets, or the old-fashioned "daisy wheel" printer, are best.

Also, the typeface should be a normal one. "Funny" faces such as italic or very small print can, again, be tiring to read.

Finally, there should be few or no hand-written corrections on the typescript. If there are lots of crossings-out, insertions, and "take-ins" (places where the author writes "takes in Page 45A," or whatever), you can get so tangled up in trying to read the manuscript that you cannot concentrate on the story.

Double-spaced

There are two reasons why manuscripts (strictly, typescripts) should be double-spaced. One is that it makes them very much easier to read. The other is that it leaves room for the editor to make corrections, as described in Chapter 9. A typical double-spaced page contains about 27 or 28 lines.

Adequate Margins

Broad margins — normally, at least an inch all round — will again make the manuscript more attractive and easier to read, as well as providing space for editing marks, questions, etc., as described in Chapter 9.

Standard Paper, One Side Only

The requirement to type only on one side of the paper may seem incredibly obvious, but believe it or not, some people still try to save money by typing on both sides of the paper or (more often) by using a double-sided photocopier. Next to hand-written manuscripts, typing on both sides of the paper is the surest recipe for making sure that no one bothers to read a manuscript.

In the United States, "standard" paper is 8.5 x 11 inches. In the rest of the world, it is A4, which is approximately 8.2 x 11.8 inches. Usually, either size is acceptable *if* the entire manuscript is typed on paper of the same size; a mixture of sizes is never acceptable. So-called "legal" paper (8.5 x 14 inches) is not usually acceptable for book manuscripts.

The paper should be clean and of good quality, typically 20-pound bond. If there are coffee-rings and dog-ears on individual pages, it suggests two things, neither of them good. The first is that the author is sloppy, and the second is that the manuscript has "been the rounds" and has been rejected several times by other readers.

Sequentially Numbered

Because a manuscript is basically just a stack of paper, it is frighteningly easy to get it out of sequence — especially if you drop it. If a manuscript is not sequentially numbered, inform the publisher or agent IMMEDIATELY, and suggest that you number it by hand. Don't even try to read the manuscript until you have done so.

Other Requirements

If you read books aimed at writers, you will encounter all sorts of authoritarian "rules" about how a manuscript should be presented; the writers of these books like to give the impression that unless these "rules" are met, the manuscript will not be read.

This is far from true. With magazine articles, it is customary (though not essential) to put both the writer's name and the name of the article on each page: this is an obvious precaution against different manuscripts being mixed up. With books, which is what you will mostly be dealing with, *some* authors add a "footer" along with the page number: for example, the "footer" at the bottom of every page of the original manuscript for this book reads "READING BOOKS AT HOME page #." Otherwise, sequential numbering is enough.

Authors' Tricks

Sometimes, when you are reading a manuscript, you will find one page upside-down or reversed (with the white side facing up and the typed side facing down), or two pages glued together, or a pair of pages out of sequence (so that the numbering might read, for example, 80-81-82-*84-83*-85-86 ...). Sometimes this is a genuine mistake, but as often as not, this indicates that you are dealing with a paranoid and amateurish author. When he gets the manuscript back, he will immediately turn to the "funny" page; and if it has not been set right way up/turned the right way round/unglued/replaced in sequence, he will immediately conclude that the manuscript has not been read, and that he is the victim of a conspiracy. I say "he" with confidence, because it seems that male writers are generally much more paranoid than women.

Before you start reading manuscripts for money, you should clear with the publisher or agent what the firm's policy is on this. Generally, it is to set the manuscript straight without comment, but there are some people who feel that dealing with paranoiacs is more trouble than it is worth, and that unless the manuscript is really good, such behavior tips the balance against the writer.

Your Responsibilities

Assuming that the author has taken the trouble to send in a good, clean manuscript, you should make every effort to keep it that way. Don't read it at breakfast and get jam on it; don't let the cat sleep on it; keep it away from small children, who might see it as drawing-paper or as raw material for a "snowball" fight using wadded up paper; make sure your hands are clean when you read it (and don't lick your fingers when you turn the pages); and, of course, don't get coffee-cup rings on it!

4.2 STORY

A good story — ah, that's why most of us read books! It's true, too, that a good story can "carry" all sorts of defects of characterization, continuity and technique (Sections 4.3 to 4.5 below). If the story is really good, then an editor will be prepared to "clean up" grammatical and other technical errors, but remember that this is *only* true if the story is very good indeed.

In a sense, the story is the simplest aspect of a book to judge. If you are caught up in the story, perhaps so much so that you do not pay much attention to the more technical aspects of the book, then it is a success. If there does not seem to be a story, or if the story is trite and predictable, then the book has problems.

A good, quick way to judge the quality of a story is to try to explain it to someone else. If there is no-one else handy, try to summarize the story on paper, in a few lines. If you can't summarize it fairly quickly, ask yourself why not. Is it because there isn't much of a story?

The "Ten Standard Plots"

As most people know, the musical *West Side Story* is effectively a re-telling of *Romeo and Juliet*. Doesn't this mean that the plot is just a rip-off?

Well, no. According to some theorists, there are only a limited number of plots in the world: some say six, some say ten, some say two dozen. The exact number does not matter: these plots have been re-used and re-hashed for hundreds or even thousands of years. The most famous is "boy meets girl; boy loses girl; boy gets girl back again." Several of Shakespeare's plots amount to little more than this — but the *story* is not the *plot*. Often, the most enjoyable books have very simple plots, if you reduce them to "Boy meets girl" terms, but the story

— the account of what happens while the plot is working itself out — is what grips us.

Also, some writers are brilliant at taking a "standard" plot and then standing it on its head, or turning it inside-out. For example, Umberto Eco's *Foucault's Pendulum* is an un-mystery story. The reader, like the protagonist, knows exactly what has happened, step by step; the plot turns on the unwillingness of the other characters in the novel to accept the obvious.

Story and Style

Remember that there is often a trade-off between "story" and "style." A really brilliant writer can keep us spellbound with an account of everyday life, but the less skill a writer has, the more the story has to carry the book.

Beware of the Message

There is a saying among experienced writers: "If you want to send a message, call Western Union." In England, the same saying is expressed as, "If you want to preach, get a pulpit."

In other words, a work of fiction is *not* the place for a message or a sermon. People buy novels to be entertained or mentally stimulated. If the book is neither entertaining nor mentally stimulating, it does not matter how worthy and "improving" the message may be: it is still a lousy book.

There are, of course, markets for such books. Unhappy schoolchildren may be forced to read them. If they are religious in character, devotees of a particular sect may be willing to buy them. Likewise, recovering alcoholics might buy a book with a strong Alcoholics Anonymous message. But even these books are failures, both as books and as vehicles for a message. If they sell only to people who already believe in the subject-matter, they can hardly be said to be spreading the message to a new audience!

This is not to say that a well-written, entertaining and interesting novel cannot incorporate a message. It is just that for every well-written book that does contain a message, there are probably a hundred and maybe a thousand that are trash.

If I have belabored this point, there are three reasons:

The first is that (badly-written) books with a message bring *all* books into disrepute. You have probably read thousands of books in your life, some good, some bad. Many people, though, read very few books. "Western Union" books will not nourish in them a love of reading.

The second is that there are a few publishers who actively seek such books, in order to sell them to a special interest groups. If you are reading for such a publisher — and they will make it abundantly clear that they *are* such a publisher — you will need to consider the "inspirational" qualities of the book alongside its other merits. If its only merit is that it promotes the "party line," say so; but if it is *also* well written and entertaining, say this as well!

The third is that it is all too easy to rate a "preachy" book higher than it deserves, simply because the writer's beliefs and prejudices agree with yours. You are a Christian, and it has a strong Christian message? You overlook the weak story and poor characterization. You are a Libertarian, and it has a strong Libertarian message? You overlook the fact that the style is leaden and plodding. You are a recovering alcoholic, or you know someone who is? You get the message.

Once again, I am *not* saying that a good book cannot have a message. Indeed, many first-class books are suffused with the writer's belief: look at C.S. Lewis's books, which strongly reflect their author's Christianity. I am just saying that a message is not a substitute for a story, and that it takes a very great writer to incorporate a message *and* write a really enjoyable work of fiction. Needless to say, there are not many writers around who are that great!

Finally, there are some excellent true stories with a very strong message: reformed drunks and drug addicts, and other accounts of those who have turned aside from the paths of wickedness. But these are not fiction, so they are dealt with in Chapter Seven.

4.3   STYLE

Style is the least definable characteristic of a book, and the most personal. Fortunately, you don't need to be able to define and analyze it, at least at first: you just have to recognize it. Like a good story, a sparkling style will mean that you are soon captivated by the book. A leaden or plodding style will have the opposite effect, just as a dull story will. Instead of neglecting other things in order to read the book, you will find excuses to stop and do something else. When you stop to call your friends, things are getting bad; when you stop to do the housework, or wash the car, there is little hope for the book!

When you read books for profit, though, you have to be able to say rather more than "I like the style" or "I didn't like the style," because you are being paid to do two things: first, to say *whether* a book is good or bad, and secondly to say *why* a book is good or bad.

Make Comparisons

A good way to analyze style is to compare the unknown writer's style with the style of a more widely-known writer. That way, the publisher or agent gets an idea of "where you are coming from."

For example, one reader might say, "I loved this book because it reminded me of Dickens: everyone in it was a real person, the sort of person we have all met." Another reader might say, "This book is like the worst of Dickens: windy, wordy, old-fashioned and moralizing." Either way, the publisher or agent can start with common ground (his own appreciation of the works of Charles Dickens) and then go on to the reader's ground (liking or disliking both Dickens and the book under review).

Although it is a good idea to do this, you *must* stick with well-known writers. You might think that a new novelist was brilliantly funny, "in the style of Thorne Smith. " Unless the agent or publisher is familiar with Thorne Smith's books, though, this won't mean much.

Try to Set a Date

When you read a book, you should have a clear sense of *when* everything happened. The style of the book should suit this. If you are reading the sort of thriller that is set one day ahead of tomorrow's headlines, it should have a 1990s feel to it. If everything about the book — the settings, the attitudes, the people and so forth — reads like a re-run of the 1960s, there is clearly something wrong. Likewise, a novel about the Pilgrim Fathers should make you feel what it was like to live in a time when religious bigotry was the norm, and the slightest deviation from prescribed behavior was savagely punished: a 1980s "Yuppie" viewpoint would hardly be appropriate.

Spot the Joins

A really well-written book is a seamless, smooth whole. A badly-written book is full of explanations, flashbacks, inconsistencies and other problems which detract from the pleasure of reading it. The writer's aim should be "show, don't tell," so that even the most obtruse and complex explanations are absorbed smoothly into the text. If you can see the "joins" where a piece of information was inserted into the text because it was unnecessary to the story, but without making the story flow smoothly, the writer is not doing his or her job properly.

As an example of "joins," I was recently reading a book set in India. The author kept using Hindi words — a common trick to lend local color — but instead of letting the context of the book carry them, each word was tediously explained. Thus, instead of saying (for example) "the old man rose from the rickety *charpoy* on which he had been sleeping," the author would write something like, "the old man rose from his rickety *charpoy*, the simple bed made of woven rope or palm on a wooden frame, on which he had been sleeping." Now, the first example doesn't tell you what a *charpoy* is, but you can guess that it's an item of furniture (or it wouldn't be rickety), and that it's something for sleeping on. What else do you need to know? The second example, by contrast, interrupts the book to give you a Hindi language lesson.

4.4 CHARACTERIZATION

Characterization is the technique of making the people in a book "come alive." It is completely separate from both story and style. Some authors can tell a riveting story, in a really gripping style, yet still have characters that are cardboard cut-outs. For "genre" books, readers generally don't care (many of them don't even notice) that the characters do not seem real: there's lots of action, lots of descriptions of places and things, and these are substitute for characterization.

Also, it is not unusual for the main character (or even two or three of the main characters) to seem "real," while the others lack reality — a lack which is all the more obvious because of the contrast between the well-written ones and the badly-written ones. A really well-written character should be almost like someone we know: we should be able to imagine the clasp of their hand, what they would say if we were introduced to them, the way they would react if they tripped over a broken paving-stone. Writing to this standard is not easy, and authors sometimes take the easy way out, giving their full attention only to some characters.

"Stock" Characters

Many writers use "stock" characters — people whom they do not need to characterize too carefully, because we already have a pretty good mental picture. Although this can be a useful "shorthand," it can also be the mark of shallow, facile writing: "genre" novels frequently use "stock" characters, such as the English Lord, the Hard-Working Nurse and the Overworked Doctor in romances; the Outsider (or Computer Nerd) Who Saves the World in science fiction; the Narrow-Eyed Gunslinger in Westerns.

Another type of "stock" character is the mark of the writer who cannot imagine more than two or three characters. For example, there are several well-known science fiction writers who may change the *name* of their principal character from book to book, and may even change his physical appearance slightly (fair or dark); but the *character* (his reactions, and even his overall build or constitution) remains constant.

Although you will usually be reading the work of new authors, who will not have had time to develop characters in this way, you may frequently find that inexperienced writers have "lifted" characters from other writers: here is the stock Robert Heinlein hero, here is the stock Barbara Cartland heroine. Using "stock" characters in this way is not necessarily bad in "genre" fiction, because the readers may well share the writer's experience and knowledge, so they can slip into a comfortable, familiar world with very little effort; but in anything that wants to rise above the world of pulp fiction, "stock" characters are bad news.

Characterization Techniques

We learn about the characters in a book from the way they react to things. There are many ways that a writer can use to show us how a character reacts, but there are four main ones. They are:

Dialog — What does the character say in response to a situation?

Internal dialog — How does the character feel about something? The clues here are words like "...he thought," or "...she wondered." This is called "internal dialog" because the character is, in a sense, debating with himself (or herself).

Physical response — Imagine a character in a bar. Someone insults him. He knocks the other person senseless. Tells you a lot about his character, doesn't it? Of course, he can always indulge in internal dialog afterwards: "Inside, Don cursed his quick temper. Now he would have to get out of town until the heat died down." Suppose, though, that he tried to make a joke of the insult? Or that he attacked the other person, but lost? This is all a part of "show — don't tell," as described above.

Expectations — We have different expectations concerning (say) a professor of philosophy and a football forward. Now make the professor an ex-football forward. We already have an idea of his appearance and thought-patterns, don't we? Or again, Spike Milligan describes a Catholic priest (I'm quoting from memory): "His powerful physic suggested a rugby player, and the broken nose confirmed it. Which goes to show how wrong you can be, because he had never played the game in his life."

With such a powerful range of tools for characterization available, it is hardly forgivable when writers don't bother!

4.5 <u>CONTINUITY</u>

There is no need to say very much about continuity — a large part of it comes under the same heading as "*Spot The Joins*" in Section 4.3 above. It is worth saying, though, that if a critical reader is unable to follow the sequence of a book, the uncritical reader is going to have even more difficulty, unless of course he or she is *very* uncritical indeed.

The best place to see failures in continuity is in detective novels, where the author neglects to give his reader some vital piece of information which the Great Detective produces with a flourish at the end of the book. For most people who read detective stories, much of the attraction of the book lies in trying to keep up with (or ahead of) the Great Detective, and if they don't have the information, they can't do it.

The very worst failures in continuity, though, are when a story line suddenly peters out. Typically, this will be in a romantic sub-plot. The writer has been told that his (or her) book must have "romantic interest," and the romantic sub-plot is essentially "tacked on" to the main story. Then, as the climax of the plot draws near, the writer literally forgets his sub-plot. At the worst, where there are several unresolved sub-plots, it can seem as if the book was cobbled together from half-a-dozen different story lines, which were left to fight it out among themselves, and the fittest survived.

A good way to spot failures in continuity is to write down the names of the principal characters as they appear, and then to tick them off as their stories are completed. If there are too many characters whose stories start but never finish, the book has problems.

4.6   **TECHNIQUE**

Technique — the basic skills of writing English — is a subject that can hardly be covered in a few words. Three things stand out, however.

The first is that spelling and grammar have a very simple purpose: they are intended to make the language easier to understand. Within reason, "wrong" spelling and grammar do not make any difference: indeed, there are times when a "wrong" construction such as a split infinitive ("to boldly go" instead of "boldly go to") is easier on the ear and easier to understand than a tortuously "correct" version. As Winston Churchill once wrote in the margin of an excruciatingly "correct" official missive, "This is the sort of English up with which I will not put." Unless there are compelling reasons for straying from the "correct" version, though, there is no reason (except ignorance or carelessness) *not* to write good English.

The second is that English has many dialects — and that the American language is not the same as the mother tongue. There are differences in spelling (color, colour; medieval, mediaeval; tyres, tires), in grammatical usage (the English don't use "gotten" except in the compound "ill-gotten"), and in vocabulary: the automobile (car) provides a useful example, with its hood (bonnet), fenders (wings), windshield (windscreen), and more. The oil pan is a sump to an Englishman or an Australian, and an oil chamber to an English-speaking Indian. Again, usages change with time: a hundred years ago, American spellings were usually the same as English ones. Whatever you are reading, remember where and when it was written. This is especially important if the writer is quoting historical material.

The third technical point is that there are some usages which are just plain wrong. One of my favorite is "prestigious," which actually means "deceitful" or "unworthy of serious regard" and comes from the same root as "prestidigitation" (= "conjuring"). *Some* American dictionaries note that is also used to mean "having prestige" or "commanding respect." It is surprising how often you can use either meaning, without altering the accuracy of the statement: "a prestigious new product." Finally, the subjunctive or conditional is disappearing from the American language: "He may have been killed by the Mafia" does *not* always mean the same as "He might have been killed by the Mafia." If he is still alive, you certainly cannot say that he *may* have been killed, but you can say that he *might* have been killed. The former expresses uncertainty as to whether he is still alive, and if he is not, as to how he died; the latter must be used if there are any conditions attached, such as "he might have been killed by the Mafia if they had found him."

In general, spelling and grammatical mistakes do not matter very much, unless they make the manuscript hard to read. On the other hand, they are at the very least the evidence of a poor education, and if someone has decided to try their hand as a writer, they should have taken steps to improve their own shortcomings. At worst, they are evidence of carelessness. A writer who is careless in grammar and spelling may also be careless in story-telling, style and characterization.

Spelling

Spelling was not really standardized until about two hundred years ago, when dictionaries first became popular. If you read Shakespeare's plays as he wrote them, you will see that many spellings are different from the modern ones, and the same is even more true of Shakespeare contemporaries (the Bard's spellings were often the ones that dictionary-writers adopted as "standard").

Even so, spelling is more or less standardized now, though there are still permitted variants: when I was at school in England, I was taught to write "standardised" with an "s" instead of a "z," and "z" is pronounced "zed" in England instead of "zee" — which makes it easier to distinguish from "c", "d", "e", "g", "p", "t" and "v". Outside the permitted variants, though, bad spelling can be a real problem *if* it is hard to understand. For example, one girl asked her father what "archeries" were. She meant "arteries."

If you have difficulty with spelling, either buy a dictionary (a good second-hand one will do; you can often get a *Webster's* for $20 or so) or get one of those electronic "spell checkers." The spell checker will, however, cost you more money and won't tell you the meanings of unfamiliar words.

Why should you worry about spelling? After all, you are not expected to grade a manuscript in the same way a teacher grades a school assignment. You *are*, however, expected to be able to tell correct English from bad English; and if your report makes no account of consistently bad spelling in a manuscript where errors are rampant, your publisher or editor may wonder about your other skills.

The Great Thesaurus Swindle

One point, closely related to spelling, that you should know about is the use of thesauruses. A thesaurus is supposed to improve your writing by broadening your vocabulary, and many of the word-processing programs used by writers today are equipped with built-in electronic thesauruses.

They are a snare and a delusion. You can always spot a writer who uses his thesaurus too much. His work is full of unusual words, which are often used slightly incorrectly, because a thesaurus never distinguishes between shades of meaning. If you find that you have to keep running to your dictionary because of the unfamiliar words, or that you know what a word means but the writer does not appear to have it quite clear, you are reading a "thesaurus special."

An example that I encountered when I was writing this was "prevaricate" for "lie." In the entry on "prevaricate" in the Oxford English Dictionary, there are many examples of the word, and it is clear from these (and from the Latin roots) that to prevaricate is to straddle or skit around the truth; never actually lying, but never telling the whole truth either. Beware of cheaper, non-scholarly dictionaries, though: they may give less accurate definitions. And, of course, a thesaurus gives no definitions at all.

Grammar

Much the same is true of grammar as is true of spelling. As long as the work is readable, a good story and good style can "carry" poor grammar. Also, many skilled writers deliberately use unusual grammatical constructions to enhance their work. There are, however, certain basic rules which should be violated only when the writer is deliberately trying to convey an ill-educated character: for example, saying "them is" (instead of "they are") or "it weren't" for "it wasn't" — though "it weren't" can be a perfectly correct subjunctive, as in "if it weren't for the decline in educational standards, this wouldn't be a problem."

Generally, though, the only grammatical mistakes that matter are the ones that you notice. If you don't notice them — if the story carries you on past them — then almost by definition, they cannot be important.

Also, don't be too ready to judge someone else's grammar by the standards of a half-forgotten high-school education. Many high-school English teachers have a "tin ear" for the rhythms and subtleties of the English language, so they bury their ignorance in a shelter of self-invented rules. Even if the rules are widely agreed upon, it doesn't mean that they cannot be broken. You may have noticed that I quite often begin sentences with "but," which is *verboten* by many English teachers. My view, though, is that sometimes a sentence is strengthened by beginning with "but." After all, it is the way we often speak, and punctuation is a way of reflecting speech and ordering our thoughts. As Humpty Dumpty said (I'm quoting from memory again), "Words mean what I pay them to mean ... it's a question of who is to be master, that's all."

Style Manuals

Some people put great value on "style manuals." The most famous is the Chicago Manual, which lays down all sorts of rules and is quite useful if your English is limited. The drawbacks of style manuals, though, are twofold. First, they lay down all sorts of rules that are irrelevant or parochial: numerous writers (and editors) are intimidated into complying with made-up rules that are neither useful nor ornamental. Second, they are no substitutes for a good "ear." A style manual is to a writer as a tuning fork is to a blues musician: its rules and strictures bear about as much resemblance to good writing as the hum of a tuning fork bears to good music.

The Role Of The Editor

I have, I hope, made it clear that if a story is good enough, spelling and grammar can be "cleaned up" by an editor. I hope that it is equally clear that unless the story is very, very good, *no* editor is going to bother to re-write it. Always bear this in mind when you are reviewing a manuscript with technical shortcomings!

4.7   DON'T PANIC

As you come to the end of this chapter, you may feel that there is far too much to do when you are reading a book for money: you simply won't be able to remember to do it all.

First of all, don't panic. It may seem as if there is a lot to remember, but all you are doing is the same as you have always done: judging a book as good or bad. The only difference is that now, you are verbalizing the reasons why you think it's good or bad.

Second, remember that you don't have to do everything at once. Quite often, I will read something twice: the first time to gain an idea of the subject, structure and overall "feel," and the second time to check on technical aspects.

Third, use this simple checklist to make sure that you have covered all that needs to be covered:

❑   STORY — What was the story? Was it well told?

❑   STYLE — Did you like the way the writer wrote? Why (or why not)?

❑ CHARACTERIZATION — Did the people seem real? How did the writer make them seem real?

❑ CONTINUITY — When you finished, were there things that you still felt needed to be explained?

❑ TECHNIQUES — Was the English readable?

4.8   SAMPLE FICTION REVIEW

This is a sample of how you might write up a review on a book you have just read:

THE HILL OF MIDNIGHT, by Vernon Miltown

At first sight, this is a fast-moving and reasonably competently written spy/adventure story. Unfortunately, at second glance it dissolves into a jumble of unrelated chapters, further marred by complete ignorance of the subject matter.

The main character is John Dunbar — I think. I say, "I think," because there are so many characters competing for the reader's attention that it is hard to be sure who is the protagonist. The characterization of John Dunbar, like the numerous other characterizations in the book, is very well handled; but unfortunately, there is no plot. In the first chapter, Dunbar is in the jungle in an unspecified Asian country, possibly Burma, on the track of opium growers; in the second, he appears to be somewhere in the South Seas; in the third, he does not appear at all; and in the fourth, he is in the author's version of Washington, D.C.; a place which bears little resemblance to the capital of the United States. As examples of the errors, the author refers to the "broad, flat back of an elephant" (has he ever looked at an elephant in a zoo?); to the towering skyscrapers between Dulles Airport and central Washington; and to swerving off a jungle track in a jeep, clearly unaware of what real jungle looks like. Also, if he wants to make much of his characters' use of firearms, he had better learn that you *cannot* fire a .44 magnum from inside your raincoat pocket.

The romantic interest (Susan Carton) is plainly an afterthought, because the writer was told that he had to have one; she disappears somewhere around Chapter 13, though her name is mentioned once more in Chapter 16 (there are 19 chapters in all). At the end of the book, the hero catches the Arab terrorist who appeared in Chapter 5 (since 1990, Arab terrorists have been flavor-of-the-month), and we are supposed to be satisfied with this as a conclusion.

If he could learn to tell a story, the author would probably be very good. I enjoyed his descriptions of people and places, and he can certainly create mood. The only trouble is that he does not know what to do with any of it. Perhaps he should try short stories as a way of focusing his attention. *Not* recommended for publication

* * * * *

Note that the reviewer has not plodded through all of the categories we listed in Section 4.7. Instead, he has concentrated on the (relatively few) strong points of the book, and on its more numerous weak points.

He has used his own general knowledge (jungles, Washington, firearms), but he could easily have got this from books or movies: he is not necessarily a globe-trotter. You might not have spotted those mistakes, but you would almost certainly have spotted others. The big problem, though, is clearly the lack of a plot, and a confused story-line.

Praise is given where it is due (characterization, mood), and not too grudgingly; but the criticism of "flavor-of-the-month" writing (the Arab terrorist) is also telling. Reading a book like this can be hard work, but it can also teach you a great deal about how *not* to write.

5.0 <u>CHILDREN'S FICTION</u>

If you have children, you probably know the sort of books they like. Because you love books, you read to your children, passing on the gift that you value so highly. If you have very young children, you probably spend quite a lot of time reading to them.

Well, how about reading to your children — and getting paid for it? That's what could easily happen, if you start reading children's fiction for money!

If your children are older and read for themselves, you also have a good idea of what they like and dislike. In fact, if they can be relied upon to look after a manuscript, they can even act as extra readers! Some children, especially the older and more mature ones (who can be as young as eight or ten, in some cases) can provide astonishing insights — and, of course, they can enjoy what they are doing. I know that I would have *loved* to have read unpublished books and pass my comments on them when I was a child. Wouldn't you?

I should, however, put in a word of warning here. If you don't have children — or at least, if you don't have favorite nieces and nephews, or the children of friends to whom you are close — you may find it difficult to judge children's fiction properly. There are some adults who have the gift of being able to understand what children want, but there are many more who do not. If you don't have that gift, which is something almost instinctive, you *must* keep in touch with children to see what interests them.

Obviously, many things for children's fiction are the same as they are for adult fiction: for example, the manuscripts must be well presented, as described earlier in Section 4.1. There are, however, some differences in emphasis, and these are the subject of this chapter.

5.1 <u>AGE CONSIDERATIONS</u>

My wife's parents, approaching eighty, refer to my wife and me as "the kids," and we are in our forties. Clearly, "children" is a flexible term!

Generally, though, children's books are divided into three broad groups. There are the ones that are written for children who are too young to read for themselves, or who need help with their reading because they are just learning; there are the ones that are written for children who are old enough to read for pleasure, but who are still interested in children's themes; and there are "young adult" books, which are transitional between children's themes and adult themes.

In practice, the different levels blend and merge, and a really well-written book can appeal to anyone of any age. When I was eight or nine, I used to read "adult" science-fiction books and magazines (a safe ground, because there is virtually no sex and very little violence in traditional science fiction!), and to this day, one of my favorite books is "Speed Six," a book about racing a vintage Bentley at Le Mans in the 1950s, written for children as young as eight or ten. For that matter, I still like Beatrix Potter almost as much as I did when I was five.

One very important point to be made here is the "controlled vocabulary" controversy. One school of educators believes that children should gradually have their vocabularies enlarged, with new words introduced in carefully graded steps. These people believe that long or difficult words should never appear in children's books.

The other school of educators says that this is nonsense, and that within reason it is good — nay, essential — for a child to be exposed to new words all the time. Otherwise, the child will find that it can get by with a stunted vocabulary, and its vocabulary will remain stunted all its life.

I am very much of the latter school — and I used to be a teacher, teaching eleven- to eighteen-year-olds. They were muttering in discontent when I handed the books out; it was old-fashioned, they said, and they couldn't understand it.

Their viewpoint changed completely when I did a simple demonstration. Choosing the prettiest girl in the class, and standing on the other side of her desk, I held her eyes with mine and began to recite from memory:

"When I do count the clock that tells the time,
And see the brave day sunk in hideous night,
Then of thy beauty do I question make,
That thou among the wastes of time must go..."

I was only twenty-three at the time, so it hadn't been too long since I was dating teenagers (or indeed, since I had learned that poem at school myself) so I could put a fair amount of conviction into my recitation. At the end of the poem, the girls were all melting and doe-eyed, and the boys had realized that Shakespeare might be of some use after all. They loved the Bard ever afterwards and, most importantly of all, they learned the power of words. They would *never* have done that from a "controlled vocabulary" book, which by definition is written by an educator rather than by a literary genius.

Books For Young Children

Books for very young children are normally heavily illustrated, and generally fall into two groups.

One is the sort which is intended to help the child to read: the old "*A is for Apple*" stuff. While such books are sometimes put out to readers, the publishers themselves normally have a good idea of what is needed, and besides, the books are so short that even an executive editor has time to read them! These are the only books where a "controlled vocabulary" is really appropriate.

A more fruitful type of book for the freelance reader is the book of nursery stories — which may be fairy stories, or adventure stories, or (a perennial favorite) stories about naughty children.

With these books, there is really no substitute for practical research; in other words, for reading the stories to the children (or, with older children, reading the stories *with* them) and seeing what they like. If you have children of the right age, you have an unparalleled opportunity to do this! All too often, books are published which *look* beautiful, and which adults find very attractive, but which are complete failures with their intended audience because they're "not interesting."

Remember, too, that there is often a considerable gap between what you think children *ought* to like and what they *do* like. Partly, this is because times change, and to some extent the whole culture changes with them: Teenage Mutant Ninja Turtles and Rambo did not exist when I was a boy, and television and movies (and life in general, for that matter) were less violent. At the same time, World War II was a recent memory and the Nazis were still favored for the role of the villains — and the Roaring Twenties were only a quarter of a century in the past, whereas now they are simply history for most people.

Another reason why children might say they don't like a book, though, is that they don't like it *right at this moment*. Tomorrow, they might like it; but for now, they would rather be at the beach, or playing Cowboys and Indians, or whatever. If you are trying books out on your children, always be sensitive to their moods. The younger they are, and the shorter their attention span, the more important this is.

Finally, remember that children have preferences, just as adults do. One child may love dinosaurs, while they leave another cold; another may be fascinated by the story of some sporting exploit (in Little League, say) while another may be vehemently opposed to any such story-line. If at all possible, try a story out on more than one child, especially if the first child does not like it. Other parents may well have children to whom they would be delighted to have you read.

Books For Pre-Teens

In many ways, the pre-teen market is the hardest to understand. This is the age when children's personal preferences really begin to show. Traditionally, little girls fall for stories about ponies, while small boys read adventure stories.

It is also the most carefully graded market — and the one where the grades mean least. Books are sold for "ages seven to eight," "ages eight to ten," and so fourth; but you will find some seven-year-olds reading books meant for twelve-year-olds, and eleven-year-olds reading books meant for eight-year-olds. In fact, the "pre-teen" market really stretches into the early teens: the reading tastes of thirteen-year-olds are not really that different from those of twelve-year-olds. The biggest single break comes at fourteen or fifteen, when young people start to notice the opposite sex. They also begin to appreciate other aspects of the outside world, and to explore interactions with it: this is the age at which they begin to realize that dreams *can* come true, if you work at them, and that their ambitions may be realizable. Understanding this is a major step towards adulthood; doing something about it is perhaps *the* major step towards adulthood. Books help you to do something about it: read Louis Lamour's *Education of a Wandering Man*.

To cap it all, different publishers have different ideas about what constitutes "juvenile fiction," and there is no question that "juvenile fiction" has become *more* juvenile over the years. If you read Victorian books for children, or even books from the 1930s, you will see that they were much more "difficult" than modern books. My own view is that if a book is really well-written, with a good story written in an interesting style, it won't matter how "difficult" it is; but if a book is badly written, it won't matter how carefully controlled the vocabulary is, because it won't be worth reading.

This market is also critical in the child's development. A child who reads well-written, interesting books at this age will develop a love of reading which will endure for the rest of his or her life. A child who is given only dull books will not grow up to be a reader.

Much of what was said about books for young children also applies to this market, and so does some of what follows in the following section. The most important thing, though, is *your* talent at spotting what young children will read — something I will come back to in Sections 5.2 and 5.3.

Books For Older Children

This is where things become *really* interesting. The teenager is part child, part adult. The childish part continues to read children's adventure stories, where action is a substitute for characterization, while the adult part becomes more interested in stories about relationships and emotions, and about the wider world — the real world, not the world of simplistic fiction.

The difficult thing for parents (and for publishers' and agents' readers) is to satisfy both of these requirements, without pushing the teenager too strongly in one direction or the other. When I was teaching in the 1970s, I was amazed at the number of books that dealt with teenage pregnancies and were apparently intended for fourteen- and fifteen-year-olds. There may well be room for a few books on this subject — there is room for books on almost any subject — but after a while, I began to wonder whether it wasn't a question of writers working out their own adolescent fantasies about teenage relationships, rather than trying to write a real book.

Quite honestly, by the time an intelligent and well-educated child is into his or her teens, he or she should be capable of reading adult books. Not *War and Peace* or Henry Miller, perhaps, but ordinary light fiction. As I have said earlier, I started reading science fiction at the age of eight or nine and, actually, these books are very suitable for children: the language is normally very restrained (especially in the older books), there is next to no sex (again, with some notable modern exceptions), and the violence is rarely excessive.

If the child is *not* well-educated, as is distressingly often the case today, he or she may require "teenage" books. A "teenage" book, in this context, must meet three criteria.

First, it must not be overly long. If a child is not ready to read adult books, he or she is unlikely to be able to handle a full-length novel.

Second, it must not be overly complex. Again, if a child cannot handle an adult book, a multi-layered plot is only going to be confusing.

Third, it must be appropriate to the child's intellectual and emotional development. This last point — emotional development — is the difficult one, because if the child is not intellectually developed, the emotional development must also be incomplete. If the book is a straightforward adventure story, essentially a teenage version of a pre-teen book, this is not much of a problem. It is when the book tries to deal with "adult" themes that life becomes difficult.

Because of the society we live in, children imagine that they are ready for emotional and, indeed, sexual relationships at a very early age. Maybe they are right; certainly, you can be just as badly hurt at forty as you can at fourteen. On the other hand, their parents do not see things that way, and the culture in which we live is just not set up that way.

Any book for teenagers that deals with emotional relationships must, therefore, walk a very fine line. On the one hand, it cannot encourage teenage sexuality. On the other hand, it must not be "preachy," or no-one will bother to read it. Somewhere between those two limits, it must try to promote an understanding of interpersonal relationships. In other words, it needs to be both encouraging and discouraging at once!

Needless to say, to write a book like this requires something like genius; and geniuses are notably rare. A really good book for teenagers is worth more than rubies.

5.2   STORY

The younger the child, the more important the story is. As a rule, children do not worry too much about characterization: a strong, simple story, preferably with plenty of action, is what they want.

As they get older, characterization becomes more important, and the plot can also get more complex, until they are reading adult fiction; this is a continuous process of evolution.

Messages

Even more than in adult fiction, you do *not* want a message in children's books. Certainly, the writer can try to incorporate a message, whether anti-drug or anti-teen-pregnancy or anything else; but the primary function of a work of fiction is to entertain. In the vast majority of cases, writers who are peddling a message are doing so in the hope of selling to the lucrative academic market. They don't care that it's a lousy book that is going to put children off reading for the rest of their lives — or maybe, they are such bad writers that they don't realize that it's a lousy book.

To realize how serious this is, think how much pleasure you get from reading. Now imagine being a child, forced to read a book by a bad writer, simply because it contains a socially acceptable message. This could easily kill a budding love of reading. You have a duty to prevent that!

5.3 STYLE

Mercifully, the "academic" novel does not exist in the children's market. "Academic" novels, in case you are not familiar with the term, are the ones that win literary prizes and are generally praised as "important," but which no one actually reads because they are convoluted, tedious, and pretentious.

In a good novel, whether it is for children or for adults, the style is always straightforward. In other words, everything in the novel contributes something to the story. The book is not a vehicle for the author to show off his wisdom: it is something to be read and enjoyed.

This does not mean that there is no place for unusual ideas and unusual words, but it does mean that unusual ideas and unusual words must be an integral part of the book. For younger children, whose experience is very limited, there is less scope to explore the limits of human experience: after all, they are still learning about everyday life. As a child gets older, though, he or she should learn to distinguish between light fiction and serious fiction.

Light fiction is mere entertainment, completely undemanding: much like the average television program, in fact. Serious fiction requires some thought from the reader: spotting references, rejoicing in the play of ideas, learning more about society and personal relationships. There is a place for both kinds of literature, but as one gets older, there is generally *more* place for "serious" fiction.

Unfortunately, "serious" fiction is rarely written specifically for children (even older children), so the best you can normally hope for is a sort of "transitional" fiction, which uses the themes and circumstances of light fiction, but mixes in a bit more intellectual stimulation.

5.4   CHARACTERIZATION

As was already suggested, characterization is normally a bonus if you find it in children's stories. In general, heroes and heroines are stainless, villains have no redeeming qualities, and the other characters are just spear-carriers. Indeed, an excess of characterization may be boring and confusing for young children, and even into their teens, children will usually construct their own version of a character from just a sketchy outline supplied by the author.

As they get older, though, they are likely to find characterization increasingly interesting. At first, characterizations may be simple: the unpleasant character who does something unexpectedly good. Later, the motive can be examined: did he do it for the "right" reasons, or the "wrong" reasons? And then, the child can learn about how characters change: doing good things for bad reasons, bad things for good reasons, some things for no reason at all. As Socrates said, "The unexamined life is not worth living."

5.5   CONTINUITY

Very young children apparently have no need of continuity. Reality and dreams are not well separated, and a story can jump around in the way that a dream does, without the child worrying in the least.

As the child gets older, though, his or her world becomes increasingly structured; and children also expect their stories to be well structured. Children are often relentlessly literal minded, and they want to know what happens — much more than they want to understand the complexities of the story. A classic example of this was furnished by my brother, who at the age of eight or ten was taken to see *A Man For All Seasons*. He slept through most of the movie, and when he woke up at the end, he asked, "Who won?" This is a fairly typical way for a child to see things, and unless a book explains clearly what happened to everyone, they may feel cheated.

So, for that matter, may adults. Jack Higgins revised his enormously successful *The Eagle Has Landed* to include "histories" of what happened to the principal characters after the main story finished. It added nothing to the dramatic impact of the novel, but interestingly, it took nothing away from it either. Perhaps we are not as sophisticated as we think.

5.6   <u>TECHNIQUE</u>

There is a great difference between simplification and oversimplification. The younger a child is, the simpler a book should be — within reason. Short sentences and straightforward language are highly desirable.

On the other hand, many authors "write down" to children (it's the same as "talking down"). If there is a *right* word that is slightly unusual, and a word that is familiar but not quite as good, they will use the familiar word. Take the phrase "to look askance." There is nothing that means quite the same. You can say, "Peter did not quite trust John's argument, though he was not sure why;" but it is neither as economical nor as elegant as "Peter looked askance at John's reasoning," nor does it convey the same air of reproach as "looked askance." Of course, "reproach" is another "hard" word.

In practice, the vocabulary that someone can *understand* is always greater than the vocabulary which they feel comfortable *using*; except perhaps in the case of very bad writers, whose dependence on their thesaurus means that they use a vocabulary greater than they understand (see Section 4.6).

To understand this, look at the way you read. If you encounter an unfamiliar word, and you cannot work out its meaning from the context in which it is used, what do you do? If it is essential to the understanding of what you are reading, you look it up. Otherwise, you let it slide by. Sooner or later, if you encounter it again, you will either look it up, or work out the meaning from the context. That is how your vocabulary grows. If you never encounter unfamiliar words, your vocabulary never grows. Now tell me that there is no place for unfamiliar words.

6.0   PLAYS AND SCREENPLAYS

As I have already made clear in Chapter 3, "The Unwritten Word," there is not much scope for reading movie scripts, and even the market for reading play scripts is not very large.

Even so, it is worth saying a little about them, partly because you may wish to specialize in the admittedly limited area, and partly just because it is interesting!

The first thing to realize is that both play and movie scripts contain surprisingly few words. They may *look* massive, because they are printed on huge stacks of paper, but each individual sheet has very little information on it. This is to make it easier for the actors to learn their lines, and for the director to follow the action.

This leads directly to the next thing that you need to realize. Much of the final production — the play or the movie — depends on the director, the actors, the set-designers. All sorts of people, as well as the writer, have a part in what the script will finally become.

With this in mind, we can look at a play or movie script in the same way that we have looked at other fiction.

6.1   STORY

Usually, the story in a play is fairly simple. I'll say "play" from now on, even though most of what I say applies to movie scripts, just because it is quicker than writing "plays and movie scripts."

It has to be fairly simple, because the story has to be told quickly. You may take several days, or even weeks, to read a book; but a play or a movie is over in an hour or two, or at most three.

A playwright must, therefore, be an expert at sketching characters quickly and accurately, and at setting the scene for what is going to happen. A play that was written with as much detail as a book would be so long that it could never be performed.

6.2   STYLE

As usual, "style" is intensely personal. As you read the script, though, remember that actors are going to have to deliver the lines that you are reading. Speak the lines out loud to yourself. Do they sound natural? The spoken word must meet quite different standards from the written word, and material which looks quite reasonable when it is written down can seem very wooden and slow-moving when it is read out loud. A play cannot afford to be as detailed as a novel; it must be much faster-moving.

At the other extreme, the text must be comprehensive enough to explain what is going on. In "method" acting, the actor tries to sound as natural as possible by basing his interpretation of the character on observations from real life. This may involve all sorts of hesitations, "umms," "errs," primal screams and gestures; but a "method" script is a contradiction in terms, because the writer has to indicate *precisely* what is wanted.

This may be done through the dialogue, or it may be done through stage directions. When you read the stage directions, though, they must (like the dialogue) sketch the essentials, rather than describing everything in detail. In the first place, you cannot hope to describe everything that must appear on the stage, or every move and gesture of the actors. In the second place, if you did, no one would ever stage the play. Not only do directors and actors like to leave their stamp on the play, they *have* to leave their stamp on it, if it is to "come alive." Otherwise, they are just robots going through a pre-programmed sequence.

6.3   CHARACTERIZATION

Much the same applies to characterizations as applies to story and to style: the writer has to be economical, and to describe the bare bones of the character in a way that fits the plot, but leaves room for interpretation.

One thing that the writer should *not* do in his attempts at characterization is to assign the part to the actor of his choice. There are several reasons why not. At the most basic, it is sheer laziness. It is all very well to say "Jack Nicholson should play this role," but by doing so the author is shifting the responsibility for characterization from himself to Jack Nicholson. Also, even if the role is brilliantly written and cries out for Jack Nicholson, Mr. Nicholson may be otherwise engaged; or may not want to play the part; or be out of favor with a particular director, not necessarily for any good reason. If the script is unplayable without Jack Nicholson, and Jack Nicholson is unavailable, the script is unplayable, period.

Also, a playwright has to steer a course between two obstacles. On the one hand, there is the Syclla of concentrating so much on the principle character that all the others are just cardboard cut-outs. On the other, there is the Charybdis of devoting so much time to the development of all the characters that the story is lost in the morass of characterization. If you want to see how a genius handled it, with a minimum of stage directions and the most economical of dialogue, re-read Shakespeare. *Macbeth* is probably a good place to start.

6.4   CONTINUITY

A play lasts only for a couple of hours or so. It therefore *has* to have good continuity. If it doesn't, the writer will not have time to tell the story he wants to tell. Unfortunately, there are many writers who do not realize this and try to put in separate sub-plots. In a play, sub-plots that involve anyone other than the main characters and (at most) two other people are a luxury. One of the greatest problems with plays from amateur playwrights is that they are simply too long.

The cure can, however, be as bad as the disease. In order to get the play down to a reasonable size, the bad playwright cuts out essential action along with the inessential. Then the plot hops around like a flea on a hedgehog, with about as much chance of enlightening the audience.

6.5   TECHNIQUE

Dialogue is not always grammatical, especially if the characters are speaking in dialect. On the other hand, there are few things more excruciating than reading badly-rendered dialect. The actor is the one who puts in the explanatory accents. He can (if he is any good) read, "Yup, I reckon it were," and make it sound like a New England farm hand. An author who writes, "Yup, Ah reckun it wurr," is merely making the script hard to read, with no redeeming advantages.

Stage directions, of course, usually need to be *more* carefully considered than almost anything else, because they have to be very precise, and grammar is an aid to precision.

6.6   STAGEWORTHINESS

Stageworthiness is something that you can learn only by going to the theater. It is perhaps curious that "stagey" is an insult in the theater, and still worse, an insult in movies: it means slow-moving, wooden, and unexciting.

If you are a devoted theatergoer — and you had better be, if you want to read scripts for money — you will be able to see how some plays "work" and others don't. If a play comes alive for you when you read it; if you can imagine seeing it on the stage (or perhaps even producing it yourself); in that case, the play is probably "stageworthy."

Because of all the other people involved in the creative process of producing a play — the director, actors, set-designers and everyone else — "stageworthiness" will always be the most subjective and elusive of all the criteria by which you judge a play. On the other hand, if you *can't* judge it (at least for yourself), or worse still if you don't know what it means, perhaps you had better stick to reviewing fiction (Chapter 4) or non-fiction (the subject of the next chapter).

7.0   NON-FICTION

Non-fiction is a massive market. Many publishers specialize only in non-fiction books and do not publish any fiction at all. They know that while non-fiction rarely earns the huge profits that a fiction best-seller can bring, it is also much less usual to lose really large sums of money. The only exception is when they are bidding against one another for the biographies of famous people, which in many cases, turns out to be closer to fiction than to non-fiction anyway.

By and large, though, non-fiction writers are given smaller advances than fiction writers (or at least, smaller advances than *established* fiction writers) and the sales of their books are more predictable: modest profits are the rule, rather than a few books earning massive profits and many books losing large sums of money.

This is why non-fiction is every bit as important as fiction. It is also true, though, that less non-fiction is put out to publishers' and agents' readers, when compared with fiction. This is because non-fiction writers usually have a good track record, and publishers trust them to come up with a good manuscript the first time. What's more, because non-fiction is very much less glamorous than fiction, only a tiny percentage of the manuscripts that come "over the transom" into a publisher's or agent's office are non-fiction.

7.1   EXPERTS AND NON-EXPERTS

You might think that in order to judge the quality of a non-fiction book you would need to be an expert on the subject it dealt with.

Well, yes and no. Certainly, most publishers would want an expert to look at a book, to judge its technical accuracy. On the other hand, they would very probably want a non-expert to look at it as well, in order to judge its chances of success. That non-expert could be you. Of course, if you do happen to be an expert in a given subject, than the expert could be you, too!

What the Subject Matter Expert Does

If the publisher knows what he is doing, the subject matter expert has one job, and one job only: to check the book for technical accuracy. Obviously, the publisher does not want to put out a book with information that is just plain wrong, or (worse still) that is dangerous. There are, however, four good reasons why a subject matter expert cannot always be relied upon to give an unbiased and accurate assessment of the book *as a book*.

First, an expert may feel that he or she would have been a better person to write the book, and so may tend to find fault with it even where no fault exists. This is a common problem!

Second, even if the expert manages to put aside personal prejudice, there are always different ways to arrange information and different things to emphasize. No two experts — and the writer should be an expert, remember, or he should at least sound like one — are likely to agree on precisely how to arrange the information, or on what sections are most important. Once again, this can lead to unfair criticism.

Third, by definition, a subject matter expert already knows all about the subject. If the writer has missed something out, therefore, the subject matter expert may not spot the omission, or he may think that it is not important, because "everybody knows" all about the piece of information that has been left out; "it's obvious." Well, maybe it's obvious to an expert, but the non-experts (that's you and me) may not have the faintest idea about the cause of the War of 1812, or the correct way to tighten a spark plug.

Finally, unless the subject matter expert is also an expert on writing, he or she may be willing to put up with a text which is all but unreadable. As long as the information is all there and all correct, bad structuring, bad technique, and just plain dull writing will not matter. In order to be an expert in anything, you have to learn to wade through really dull material!

What the General Reader Does

Unlike the subject matter expert, the general reader's job is to assess the quality of the book *as a book*. As it happens, I can give an excellent example of this from recent personal experience.

I thought it might be a good idea to use one of the "on-line information utilities" that are available to anyone with a computer and a modem. For a writer, these "utilities" can be very handy, as they allow you to search through magazine references, airline databases, and much more.

I therefore went out and bought a book on personal computer communications. On the cover, there were several favorable reviews; I thought it had to be a good book.

I was totally and utterly wrong. It is unreadable. It was written *by* computer nerds, *for* computer nerds. Worse still, all the reviews were by computer nerds, too. I don't even speak the language they use. Even if I did speak their language, the structure of the book is very bad. Instead of telling you what you can find out, and where you can find it, they instead tell you what each computer system can do. I still don't even know if these "on-line utilities" would be any use to me!

If the publishers had sent this book out to any reasonably intelligent general reader — to me, or to you — they would have been told of these shortcomings immediately. But they didn't, and the result is a book which is completely useless to anyone who wanted *information* instead of a computer manual. I'm still angry about that book, which cost me $14.95, and which is printed on paper so thick that I wouldn't even want to hang it on a nail behind the outhouse door.

What, then, does the general reader look for? In essence, three things: content, structure, and readability.

7.2   CONTENT

There is an old saying in the newspaper business: opinion is cheap, but facts are expensive.

This is very true. In order to get facts, you have to do one of two things. Either you hire a writer who is willing to do the research that is needed to discover the facts, or you hire a writer who is old enough and experienced enough to know the facts without looking them up. Any fool, on the other hand, can write opinions.

Again, I can give an example from a book I read recently. It was supposed to be about living in France — the practicalities of everyday life. Well, it had some practicalities. But (for example) it had virtually nothing to say about French income tax or property taxes. It said very little about shopping hours, or about what was available in the shops. Its information on using imported electrical equipment in France was flatly wrong in several places. *All* of this sort of information should have been in the book, and it wasn't. Also, it was very parochial. "English people," it said, "cannot imagine the large distances that are common in France, where you may have to drive ten miles to buy a loaf of bread." Nonsense! There are places in England where you have to drive that far; what the authors meant was that for Londoners like them, accustomed to everything being in walking distance, the distances were large. To an American, of course, the distances are laughably small.

High-Grade and Low-Grade Facts

To fill the book up, the authors of this appalling book on France used both opinions and what I call "low-grade" facts. "Low-grade" facts are the kind of thing that you can quickly and easily find out from an encyclopaedia or a high-school history text, stuff that is easily copied out from readily available source material. "High-grade" are the kind of facts that you buy a specialized book for.

With all due modesty, I would say that there were plenty of high-grade facts in this book. What you paid for — and what you are getting — is real information on how to read books critically, so that you can sell your expertise to publishers and agents. You are also getting information on how to approach publishers, and even a partial listing of which publishers to approach. It is only a partial listing, though, for two reasons. One is that publishers' addresses are readily available elsewhere, in *Literary Market Place* and *Writers Market* (both of these are discussed at greater length later in the book). The other is that there are *so many* publishers and agents that you could write to. It is simply impossible to put them all in one book like this, while still leaving room for the "how-to" information that is *not* available elsewhere.

Completeness and Conciseness

Now that I have distinguished between "high-grade" and "low-grade" facts, it is time to look at completeness and conciseness.

Ideally, if we wanted to find out about the subject, we would read a book which told us everything we wanted to know, without any surplus information, but without omitting anything.

Unfortunately, that is impossible. Take this book as an example. Very few people are going to find much use for Chapters 3 and 6, which deal with what I have called "the unwritten word." For most of my readers, therefore, these sections are surplus information.

If I had left those chapters out, though, I would have laid myself open to the just complaint that I had omitted information which might be useful for some people. I therefore included them.

Then again, I have said nothing in this book about the process of learning to read, or about the history of the alphabet. This is because I judged that the former was irrelevant — anyone who is reading this book already knows how to read, so I do not need to start at quite that low a common denominator — and that the latter was not only irrelevant, but also a "low-grade" fact that is readily available at your local library in, say, the *Encyclopaedia Britannica*. Try, on the other hand, to find information on reading books for money in the *Britannica*!

Fortunately, there are two ways of dealing with modest amounts of surplus information in a book. One is simply to ignore them, and the other is to read them as a matter of general interest. If there is too much surplus information, though, the book will not sell because it is "overkill." To return to the example of the *Britannica*, no-one is going to spend $1500 or more on an encyclopedia, just to get one entry, but they might spend $9.95 (or even $49.95) on a book which consists *mostly* of the information they need, along with a small amount of excess information. In general, the more you charge for a book, the more focused that book has to be.

What I have tried to do in this book is to strike a balance between "core" information, which really could not have been left out, and "extra" information which may or may not be immediately useful to all my readers, but which will not actually detract from the book even if you do not find it personally useful. At the very least, you will learn a great deal of background that will be useful in establishing credibility in the publishing world. At best, you will find a use for everything in here.

To sum up, any non-fiction book must strike a balance between completeness and conciseness. Too much completeness, and large parts of the book are irrelevant. Too much conciseness, and the information you need is not in the book.

7.3 STRUCTURE

Imagine looking at the photographs of a friend's vacation; it is something that has happened to most of us at one time or another. We know that there are two kinds of presentations.

Sometimes, we are handed a huge wad of pictures, in no particular order. The friend leans over our shoulder saying, "That's me and Myrtle in Paris — no, wait, that's London. Anyway, here we are just before we set out — just look at all that luggage. Then we're in Rome, see, there's the St. Peter's. Yeah, and that's London again — no, sorry, that really is Paris. That's the restaurant we were going to have lunch in, but it was closed, so we went to another place, only we haven't got a picture of that..." When we have finished going through them, we have absolutely no idea of where our friends went, or for how long, and we are not even too sure that they are our friends anymore.

The other kind of presentation gives us a carefully edited selection of the best pictures, arranged in order (better still, in an album) in a way that gives us a quick, attractive history of their trip, from the time they set out to the time they got home. Because everything is in order, the travelog that accompanies the pictures is concise and to the point. We come away envying them their vacation, and wishing that we could afford to do the same.

Which kind is more attractive? The second kind, obviously. And what is the difference? The answer lies in one word: STRUCTURE. Structure is just as important in a book as it is when you are telling a story, or showing someone your vacation snaps.

Structuring a book properly is more than half the battle. If the structure is clear and logical, then any reasonably competent writer can simply "fill in the blanks," and flesh out the bare bones of the outline. If the structure is *not* clear and logical, then the book will be a mess.

There are many kinds of structure, but generally, successful books are structured in one of two ways. Either they are chronological, or they are thematic.

Chronological Structures

A chronological structure is one that follows a historical event from start to finish — just like our friend's vacation. It normally works for all "historical" accounts, whether they are accounts of the things we normally think of as history (the Civil War, the invention of the atom bomb), or accounts of recent events that we can all remember — or indeed, which may not yet have finished. For example, an account of the recent Savings and Loan scandal would be well served by chronological structuring, possibly even beginning with a historical section that explained how banks failed during the Depression.

Although thematic structures look very easy, they sometimes present problems. For example, one thread of the story may start before another has finished. Should the writer interrupt the first story to bring in the second one, or should he (or she) finish the first story, and then go on to the second story? The answer is that either approach can work — but whichever approach the writer chooses, the reader should not be able to "see the joins" (Section 4.3). If you can "see the joins," the writer has, to a greater or lesser extent, failed to tell the story well.

Thematic Structures

Thematically structured books are based around a series of themes. Thematic structures are suited, for example, to "how-to" books. This is a thematically structured book.

In one sense, a thematic structure is also chronological. Each section has to build on the sections that have gone before. For example, Chapter 5 ("Children's Fiction") clearly owed a lot to Chapter 4, "Reading Fiction" — and at the end of Section 7.3, "Chronological Structures," I referred back to Section 4.3.

The difficulty with thematic structuring, though, lies in how the writer chooses the themes. There is no doubt that some writers are very much better at this than others, but there is equally no doubt that no two writers will slice their subject matter in exactly the same way. Often, you will think that someone has left something out, only to find that it appears a few pages later in a slightly different place from where you expected. When you are writing a report on a book, remember this!

Structures for Special Applications

Two special examples of thematic structuring are alphabetical structuring (as found in encyclopedias) and instructional structuring. Alphabetical structuring is thematic insofar as each entry deals with a theme, but there is no overall logical structure dictated by the subject matter itself: opening my *Britannica* at random, I find Pendleton, Oregon next to Pen Drawing.

With instructional materials, the structure must be dictated by the theme, but each theme is broken down into a simple logical sequence so that the reader can work through the examples on his or her own. Writing instructional materials is a highly skilled technique in its own right, and one which few authors ever master.

Once again, an example makes this clear. Years ago, radar technicians used to be trained by telling them what would go wrong if a particular part of the radar set failed — this tube, that connection, the resistor over there.

The way they were tested, though, was quite different. They were given a broken-down radar set, and asked what had gone wrong. Usually, they could not tell you. This was despite the fact that they had been trained by some of the finest men in the field, radar experts who could make a radar set do anything *including* whistle "Yankee Doodle Dandy."

The reason for their failure was simple. They were being trained in one "direction" (this part fails, what is the fault in the set?", but they were being tested in the other "direction" (here is the fault in the set, so which part has failed?). As soon as their training was re-arranged so that the training matched the questions — as soon as they were taught to work from set failures rather than from component failures — the pass rate went up dramatically. You can see why the problem arose in the first place. In the classroom, it is easier to work from component failure, but in real life (almost by definition) you do not know which component has failed. To the instructors, who knew the subject inside-out, the two problems were effectively identical (if A causes B to fail, then if B has failed, A must be the reason). The trainees, though, did *not* know the subject backwards — but they *were* being taught it backwards. This is an excellent example of the need of structured training materials!

Mixed Structures

It is quite possible to have a thematic structure in which each theme is dealt with chronologically, and it is conceivable that you could have a basically chronological structure in which each theme is dealt with in full in the historical order in which it appeared. Certainly, some computer repair manuals deal with the different computer models in the order in which they were introduced (chronological structuring), and then the repair information is thematic/instructional.

7.4 <u>READABILITY</u>

"Readability" is the non-fiction equivalent of the fiction-writer's style — indeed, it is a form of style in its own right.

In general, the most readable non-fiction books are the ones that are written in a straight forward, person-to-person style. The best advice that a non-fiction writer can have is to write as if he or she were explaining something to a friend. A conversational tone is generally best, and the language should be as simple as possible. After all, the reader is trying to understand a new subject, and if the writing gets in the way of that understanding, the book is not as effective as it might otherwise be.

Note, though, that I say that the language should be as simple *as possible*. There is always a limit to how far it can be simplified, and the writer should not be afraid to use the correct technical terms whenever necessary. Even breathtakingly complex subjects can be handled if the writer can think clearly enough. For example, Stephen Hawking is one of the greatest physicists of all time, and the themes he deals with in *A Brief History of Time* are *very* complex, but the book remains readable. Trying to make a subject *too* simple will often result in a book which is neither informative nor easy to understand.

<u>Two Kinds of Dullness</u>

Almost never can dullness be excused, except perhaps in the most complicated and rarified texts on philosophy, the higher reaches of science, and a few other subjects — and these are not the books that should be sent out to general readers, because they are intended *only* for a few academics.

There are, however, two kinds of dullness, and it is important to distinguish between them. There is dullness of subject, and dullness of style.

Dullness of subject simply means that you are not interested in the book. For example, I can imagine few things more dull than a book about knitting. But this is because I have no interest in knitting. If you are interested in knitting, the same book would probably not be dull for you.

Dullness of style is when we find a *subject* interesting, but not the author's treatment of it. This is much more serious! Again taking a personal example, I am very interested in the history of 35mm cameras (a highly specialized subject), and I will read almost any book on the subject. If I find the author's style dull, it must be *really* bad, because I will put up with a lot to learn more about this topic.

When you are writing reports on books, always take great care to distinguish between these two different problems. A book where you find the subject dull will be harder to "fix" than a book where you find the style dull (in fact, it may be impossible to make it interesting for you), but a book where you find the style dull is more of a problem for the editor, because often, nothing short of a complete rewrite will make the book readable.

7.5   TECHNIQUE

Technique, in the sense of spelling and grammar and English usage generally, is often more of a problem in non-fiction books than in fiction. In a novel, a good story can sometimes "carry" bad technique, and if the technique is so bad that the story is almost unreadable, the book will be rejected anyway.

In a non-fiction book, though, the *information* may be perfectly sound, but the *presentation* may be awful. Often, you are not reading the words of a professional writer: you are reading the words of a subject-matter expert, who may or may not be able to write.

The most common fault is "dressing up" the language with long words and convoluted constructions because the writer believes that this sounds more important and literary. Classic examples include "at this moment in time" for "now" and "The wrench should be taken in the left hand" for "Take the wrench in your left hand."

This comes back, in effect, to the point I made in Section 7.4 about a straightforward, conversational tone. As you read a manuscript, mentally see if it could be simplified without changing the sense. If it could, say so in your report!

If there are other problems with grammar or with spelling, you should also make an assessment of how much re-writing will be required to make the text acceptable as a piece of English. Generally, you need not comment on occasional mistakes — everyone makes those, in the heat of the moment when they are writing quickly — but if there are errors in just about every paragraph, you should say so.

7.6   CHILDREN'S NON-FICTION

The rules for children's non-fiction are much the same as the rules for adult non-fiction, with one important additional consideration.

Non-fiction depends on facts. Fiction depends on imagination. Now, while no child of (say) eight years old may well know more facts than another eight-year-old, the variation in factual knowledge is not likely to be anything as great as the variation in imagination. It is therefore possible to say of a work of non-fiction, with much more confidence than you could say it for a work of fiction, "this book is suitable for eight-year-olds (or ten-year-olds, or whatever)."

Also, if a child is "ahead of himself" academically, this is no problem. I have taught fifth-graders who could handle sixth-grade and even seventh-grade mathematics without difficulty; but this did not diminish the fact that the books they were using were still suitable for *most* sixth-graders or seventh-graders.

When you are assessing non-fiction for children, you will want to remember that you are dealing with factual information. It will, therefore, be important for you to keep in mind the age of the children the book is supposed to reach, and just how much information this age group has been taught. A non-fiction book which consistently adheres to information aimed at its target readers' age will be much better received than text which jumps from facts an 8-year-old can understand to information only only a 12-year-old has been taught.

7.7   SAMPLE NON-FICTION REPORT

The following is an example of a well-written report:

COMET CATASTROPHE, by Roger Sutherland

Comet Catastrophe is an exploration of the history of comets: what they are, where they come from, and whether there really is any relationship between the appearance of a "hairy star" in the sky and natural or other catastrophes.

Although the author's approach could hardly be called scholarly, it is remarkably rigorous for a book of this type: he has apparently researched his facts carefully, and there are few if any of the third-hand (and fourth-rate) researches based on previous books of the "Chariots of the Gods" variety. Where theories are at variance with the facts, it is the theories which go, not the facts — a welcome change!

It is clear, though, that he intends this to be a popular book. Rather than completely spoil his thesis (which he admits is weak at best), he weasels out with a lot of "Could it be...?" and "No-one knows for certain if..."

He is clearly English: the constructions and spellings give that away. He also seems to be reasonably well educated, though not a professional astronomer.

The book is well structured, but a significant drawback is that it was apparently written just *before* the last apparition of Halley's Comet, and there is too much on this subject. Quite honestly, the book is fairly marginal (it might have been otherwise if it had been printed at the time of the comet), but given the willingness of people to believe in all sorts of mysticism, I believe that it could, with a minimum of editing, be made to fit into a "New Age" list.

8.0   OPPORTUNITIES AT THE WRITING STAGE

So far, I have concentrated on opportunities for publishers' readers and agents' readers — but there are many other opportunities for people who love books, understand the publishing business, and want to work at home. In this chapter, I deal with the opportunities that exist at the writing stage — including even writing your own books!

Contrary to popular opinion, writing is *not* necessarily a solitary activity, especially in the case of non-fiction. I have written many, many non-fiction books, and often I simply could not have done them without assistance. Much of my support comes from my wife, who is an accomplished photographer and researcher in her own right, and who can also draw illustrations for my books, but I have also called upon countless other friends and acquaintances.

Before going any further, I should warn you that helping a writer with a book is not a "get-rich-quick" scheme that requires no skill or experience. You do need basic skills (though this book will tell you how to hone them), and at first, you will not make much money — before you can hit the big time, you will have to establish a "track record." On the other hand, you will very likely have already one or more of the skills that are desirable in this part of the book, and it does not take long to establish a track record. Once you have, the rewards can be quite good. For example, simple line drawings will normally pay anything from $15 to $50 each, and they should not take you more than a couple of hours each. Half a dozen drawings — a day and a half's work, at the outside — could well earn you $100, $200 or even more.

One of the most common problems a writer faces is finding illustrations for his or her books, so this is a good place to start.

8.1   ARTWORK AND ILLUSTRATION

Illustrations in books are normally divided into five groups, from a *printing* point of view. I stress "printing" because the *content* of the four types of illustration can vary widely, and indeed the content may well be capable of being represented in more than one way. For example, maps might be line drawings, spot color, half-tones, or full-color renderings; or they might even be photographs of old maps "lifted" from books a hundred years old or more.

Because very few writers are also illustrators, a writer who needs a book illustrated is almost always desperate for good illustrative material. You can supply this in two ways: as an originator, which is this subject of this section, or as a picture researcher, which is one of the subjects of Section 8.2.

Tables and Charts

Many types of information are best presented graphically, and even where graphics are not strictly necessary, they are sometimes introduced to break up the monotony of solid text.

The two most usual types of charts are bar charts and pie charts. Such charts can be produced in many ways, but the three most usual are as follows:

Traditional — In the "bad old days," such charts were drawn using rulers, compasses, and Indian ink. This is slow and messy, but if you already have the necessary tools and skills, you will not have to invest any money. Even if you use modern graphic arts materials (see below), you are still likely to need some skills with the drawing pen in order to "finish off" work.

Using Modern Graphic Arts Materials — If you are familiar with modern graphic arts materials, you will find that there are all kinds of products which will make simple graphics even simpler to produce. The most important are self-adhesive colored films (or black films) and tapes, and rub-down instant lettering. Rub-down lettering, such as is made by Letraset or Meccanorma, can also be used to produce highly professional-looking charts.

Using a Computer — There are many "graphics" packages which can be used with a computer to create almost any type of artwork — and to create it to a very professional standard. The quality and complexity of graphics that you can produce will depend on the power of your computer, the power of your software, the quality of your printer (laser printers are best, but Canon's "bubble-jet" printers are very nearly as good) and, of course, your own skill.

When you are producing graphics, no matter what technique or techniques you use, it is normal to make the graphics somewhat larger than they will be in the final reproduction, so that errors and imperfections are reduced in size, rather than being enlarged. You must not work *too* large, though, or when things are reduced, line thicknesses may be reduced to almost nothing, and lines that are too close together may merge and "block up." Normally, most artists work "half up" (150 per cent the size of the final reproduction, or half as large again, so that one inch in reproduction is one-and-a-half inches in the artwork), though they may work "two up" (200 percent, twice the final reproduced size) for some kinds of work. "Three up" is normally the very biggest that is possible to work with.

Line Drawings

In printing, it is easy to get either a solid black (using ink) or a solid white (leaves the paper blank). What you cannot easily do, though, is to create a gray, known to printers as a "half tone."

A line drawing, therefore, is a drawing which consists *only* of black and white. As well as lines, there may be solid black areas, and there may even be "hatched" or "shaded" areas to create the impression of gray — though if you look closely at the "hatched" area, you will be able to see that it is made up of black lines or stippling on white, rather than being an even gray.

From a graphical point of view, producing simple line drawings is much the same as producing bar charts and pie charts, and it can be done in much the same ways — with pen and ink, with specialist graphic products, and with a computer.

More complex line drawings, of people or places or things, require more skill (and command proportionately more money). I have personally paid anything from $15 to $25 for simple line drawings, and I know of times when publishers have paid $100 or $200 or even more for skilled and complex line drawings. Is this a skill you already have? Or is it one you could acquire? It is surprising how fast your drawing skills can improve if you practice regularly.

Spot Color

"Spot" color is the simplest way of printing color. Like line drawings, "spot" color does not use half tones. This paper is simply run through the press several times, using different colored inks. The first run is usually black, and with "two-color spot" the second color is usually blue or red, though it can be any color you like. A familiar example of "spot" color might be a Santa Claus illustration in a newspaper. The basic illustration is black, and during the second run through the press, the red of his suit and hat is added. The cover of this book was printed using "spot" color, black and a second color.

Spot color illustrations are effectively line-drawings, broken up into different colors. Each color is drawn on a single clear acetate sheet, and the sheets are then stacked one on top of the other to create the whole image. Sticking with the Santa Claus example, the first acetate sheet (or "foil") would have the face, hands, boots, beard and belt, to be printed in black and white, and the second foil would have the suit and hat to be overprinted in red.

If you are not too clear on how this works, don't worry. As I said at the beginning of this chapter, this is not a "get rich quick" scheme, so if you don't have this particular skill, just forget about it. There are plenty of other opportunities for making money at home. If you *do* understand it, though, or if you believe you could master it (borrow a book on illustration from your library), it can be another string to your bow.

Half Tones and Photographs

In order to produce shades of gray in a picture for printing, the original illustration has to be "screened." Screening is a process which breaks the image up into tiny, tiny dots. In areas where the gray is darker, the dots are larger; in areas where the gray is very pale, the dots are tiny and barely visible (they are always the same distance apart, between centers).

Half tones are used to reproduce black and white photographs, and also to reproduce continuous-tone illustrations. For example, a pencil drawing contains a wide range of tones, and in order to reproduce it in print, it is "screened" just like a black and white photograph.

I will not say anything more about continuous-tone drawings — either you have that skill, or you don't, and there is not room to say much about it here — but because I expect that plenty of my readers will be reasonably skilled with a camera, I will say a bit more about black and white photographs.

Black and white photographs for books are either specially shot ("commissioned") or they are selected from existing material ("stock"). Although I can take photographs myself, there have been times when I have commissioned pictures, usually to save time or to save travelling. Specially-commissioned pictures are normal in "how-to" books, especially if they are of the "step-by-step" variety.

Needless to say, in order to shoot commissioned pictures, you need to have high-quality apparatus and to be a master of the photographic process — usually, including your own black-and-white printing. Pictures are normally presented as 8x10 inch prints, and they should be of lower-than-usual contrast, with as much of the critical detail as possible in the light and mid tones, because these are the tones that reproduce best in books.

"Stock" pictures must be of the same technical quality, and they must be clear and sharp, with no messy backgrounds. If someone wants pictures of Ford Mustangs, for example (a picture request I had to fill recently), the pictures should each show a single car against a clear background (grass is ideal). The writer does *not* want guide-ropes, people lounging with soft drink cans in the shot, prize-winning rosettes, or hand-lettered signs with the history of the car: worse still would be disembodied arms and legs protruding into the frame. These are the snapshots that anyone could take. Also, the captions must be clear and concise, especially the year in the case of a car. A good caption (which you have to write) might read,

"Ford Mustang convertible, 1966, 289 cid engine, photographed at Visalia, California, property of John Smith of Bakersfield, CA. Please credit [Your name here]."

To learn more about opportunities for photographers, read the annual *Photographer's Market*, published by Writer's Digest Books. Just to give you a guide, I recently paid someone $900 for 45 pictures, most of them from the photographer's existing stock; the rewards can be significant.

Full Color

Like half-tones, full color may be derived from artwork ("rendering") or from photographs. As you have probably guessed by now, the technology of full-color printing is a combination of the techniques for spot color and for half-tones; that is how all the different shades of the various colors are reproduced. The vast majority of full-color printing is done on four-color presses, and the four inks used are cyan, magenta, yellow and black. The original images (whether artwork or photographs) are "scanned" or "separated" to create four different black-and-white films corresponding to the four printing colors, and "screened" like half-tones to create the dots that are needed for printing. If you hold a strong magnifier over a color picture in a book, or better still, a newspaper (where the dots are coarser) you will see how the process works.

If you are photographing color for reproduction, it is normal (though no longer essential) to use slide film, and to select transparencies that are slightly darker than usual, as these give the best color. General rules for captioning and composing are the same as for black and white.

Once again, you need to read books on photography to learn how to make money this way, but I can tell you that I know two photographers who work together, and whom I know have earned $500 to $1000 a day *each* for illustrating cook-books in a "studio" in a regular domestic garage!

Copying and "Lifting" Pictures

One other way that photographers can make money is by copying old illustrations from out-of-copyright books. For example, I have an 1880s copy of "Battles and Leaders of the Civil War," which is full of engravings, maps, and even a few photographs, all of which are now out of copyright. This is an invaluable archive for illustrating books about the Civil War! All you need is a simple copying stand, a good camera with a copying lens (I favor the Micro Nikkor on a Nikon), and a couple of cheap floodlights.

8.2   RESEARCH

The difficulty here lies in finding writers with enough money to pay you! It does happen, though. In particular, if you have specialist knowledge *and* are good at using a library, writers may want to use your skills to save them time and aggravation in finding out where information is. As I write this, for example, I had recently requested help in finding information on secret societies!

Factual Research

The way in which you work with a writer will vary widely. Some writers apparently like to have photocopies made of relevant material; others want you to write a brief summary on it; and yet others want only the barest information, the place where it was published, the publisher, the author, and the date.

As with many other opportunities in this chapter, it's a field where it may take you time to get up to speed — though the more experience you get, the easier the job will be *and* the more you can charge. It will never make you rich, but even the most impecunious writer is likely to pay more than minimum wage (some publishing houses will pay a good deal more), and it is interesting work in agreeable surroundings.

Picture Research

Picture research consists of going to libraries and museums, and finding the sort of pictures that a writer needs to illustrate his or her work. Like factual research, it is a job that takes some learning, but it is also very interesting — or at least, it can be, though you may begin to wonder about this when you are faced with *seventy volumes* of Civil War photo albums, as my wife and I once were on a book that we were researching.

8.3 COMPUTER CONSULTANCY

This may seem like an odd way to earn money from writers, and as far as I know, no one is doing it yet. The thing is, though, most writers today use computers — my wife and I own five between us — and most of them are not getting the most out of them that they could.

Certainly, I would like more information on hardware selection; software selection; data transfer (including fax cards and modems); and on-line information services. What is more, I want that information from someone who understands *writing*. Usually, the people who know the answers to all the questions are hobby-oriented (to be polite) or complete computer nerds (to be accurate), and they can't get it through their heads that I don't want to play games on my computers, I use them only for word processing on Wordstar (and for doing my accounts on Lotus 1-2-3), and I'm not interested in technicalities: I just want to know what buttons to press, in order to get the results I want.

You couldn't earn a fortune (you'd probably need to advertise in writers' magazines, and give seminars at writers' conferences), but you could make a good few bucks — I would guess $50 to $100 for individual consultancies, maybe more, and $350 to $500 for seminars. Good luck!

8.4 WHY NOT WRITE A BOOK?

This is not primarily a book for writers, but by now, you must have begun to suspect that you could write a book yourself. You may well be right, especially if you have a good, original idea for a non-fiction book.

The process by which a book is born is made clear in Chapter 2, and with the information in this book, you will be very much better placed than the average would-be writer if you want to approach a publisher. The best approach is as follows:

Write a Proposal/Outline

My book proposals normally have (1) a cover sheet; (2) a selling page, where I put forward the ideas for the book and describe why I think it will sell (including an analysis of the competition); (3) a brief biographical page, which in my case also includes information on previously published books; and then (4) a chapter-by-chapter outline, which may run to one, two, or three pages, depending on how much I need to say about the contents of each chapter.

Write some Sample Text

It is always a good idea to write at least some sample text before you try to sell a book, for three reasons. The first is to prove to yourself that you can. Even experienced writers sometimes find that there is less to say about an idea than they had imagined. The second is to "write yourself in" to the project: after a couple of thousand words of sample text (the least you should do), you may find that you want to make changes to your outline, now that your thinking is more focused. The third is so that you can send sample text, along with the outline, to any publisher who expresses interest after the next stage, which is:

Write to Publishers

This is the time consuming part, and it can be the disheartening part: you *will* get rejections. Never mind: just send it out again! What you need is a one-page selling letter, similar in content to the proposal page of your proposal/outline, which will pique the publisher's interest and make him want to see more. Once you sell the book, the hard part starts:

<u>Work Like a Dog and Earn Very Little Money</u>

Well, that's the way it feels sometimes, especially when you are starting out. Writing *is* hard work, and you *do* work long hours. But there's no commuting involved, and I'll tell you this: I've been a schoolteacher and a telephone exchange operator; a beach-guard, and a ditch-digger; an accountant, and a truck driver; an advertising photographer, and a factory hand. And I'd rather be a writer than any of them.

9.0   <u>OPPORTUNITIES AT THE EDITING STAGE</u>

Copyeditors, proof readers, indexers, "blurb" writers: most publishers are permanently short of people who can do these jobs well. As I explained in Section 1.1 An Occupation for Gentlemen, many people take full-time jobs in publishing at very poor salaries, because it is "an occupation for gentlemen." Because salaries are poor, people are always moving from one publisher to another in an attempt to better themselves. This means a high turnover of salaried staff, and it means that freelance staff — people like you, if you have (or can acquire) the right skills — are very highly sought after.

Doesn't it also mean that freelances are underpaid? Actually, no. There are two big differences between salaried staff and freelances. One is that salaried staff have to be paid 365 days a year (366 in leap years!), while freelances need only be paid when there is work for them. The other is that freelances involve no overhead for the publisher: no office space (with its attendant heating, lighting and air conditioning), no support staff such as secretaries and switchboard operators, no payroll tax, no furniture, no phone bills, no photocopiers, no pension plan, nothing. And, if the work runs low, there are no problems with layoffs and severance payments.

<u>You Reap the Rewards!</u>

Because it is cheaper to hire freelances, a publisher can afford to pay freelance staff proportionately more than salaried staff. Let's say that they would pay a salary, for a particular job, of $1500 a month. That's $75 a day for 20 working days a month (take out the weekends and vacations). Overheads such as office rent, pension plans, etc., are likely to add at least another one-third to this cost, and can easily add as much as fifty per cent. Even at one-third, that's $25 extra, or $100 a day. And remember, that $100 a day has to be paid every working day.

If the publisher can pay a freelance the same $100 a day, he is already ahead: by definition, the freelance is hired *only* when there is the work to justify hiring him or her. In fact, it's better than that, both for the publisher and for the freelance. A skilled freelance may well be *more* skilled and *more* reliable than a salaried staff member. More skilled, because he or she has a wealth of experience with different books and writers and publishers, and more reliable because a freelance can't call in sick because the surf is up.

Of course, the publisher is not going to volunteer to pay a freelance writer $150 or $200 or more a day, nor could a beginner expect to earn that sort of money. At first, you will have to prove yourself. But once you have established a working relationship with a publisher, and have shown that you are skilled and reliable, a thousand bucks a week should not be out of sight. That's not bad money by anyone's standards!

This Is Where The Opportunities Are!

Although the opportunities for publishers' readers and agents' readers are considerable, they pale next to the opportunities for good freelance staff. The amount of money that you can earn is controlled by *your* skills, *your* enthusiasm, and the amount of time that *you* are willing to put in. Many freelances work very hard for weeks or even months at a stretch, with virtually no time off. Then, with perhaps $10,000 in the bank, they take off for a break — maybe in Europe, maybe in the South Seas, maybe in India.

They can do this because they work for two or three or even five or ten publishers, juggling the work to fit it all in, so that they are working harder, and for longer hours, than salaried employees — but, of course, for a much higher hourly rate! This gives them the choice of more money and more possessions, or more time to devote to what they like to do, whether it is traveling, gardening, rodeo riding, photography — or writing!

The Ultimate In Flexibility

Maybe, though, you don't want to work like that; you would prefer a gentler pace of life, and a more even way of doing business. Maybe you *can't* work like that: you already have another job, and freelance work is just a way to earn some extra money, or you have children who keep you at home. No problem!

Freelance work normally comes in "chunks," which may last for as little as a few days, or may run for several weeks. As long as you complete each job satisfactorily, and as long as you do not drop out of sight for so long that people forget about you, the amount of work that you do is up to you. You can pick and choose, doing the work that you are most comfortable with at the pace that suits you best.

Time Is Of The Essence

One thing that is ESSENTIAL to realize, though, is that copyediting, proof reading, indexing and, in fact, *any* editorial services are time sensitive. This means that you have a deadline — and you had better be able to stick to it. For all that publishers sometimes lollygag around for weeks, months or even years, they expect everyone else in the chain to be super-prompt. Once you are established, you will get a feeling for urgency: sometimes, a day or two may not matter, but at other times, it will. If you are not one hundred percent reliable when it comes to deadlines, you will soon acquire a very bad reputation and you will find it difficult or impossible to get work.

9.1   COPYEDITING

When a publisher receives a completed manuscript and passes it for publication, it usually needs a certain amount of "cleaning up." The copy editor is the person to whom the "clean up" is entrusted. He or she will be checking seven main areas. These are unresolved questions; lack of clarity; inconsistencies; spelling; grammar; punctuation; and "house style." Before looking at each of these in turn, though, there are two very important points to make about copy editing.

The first is that it requires a good general education and a clear grasp of good English. This does not mean that you have to have a college degree in English — many excellent copy editors do not. It does mean that you need to be clear on the rules of grammar, on spelling, and on all the technical aspects of the English language. You need not necessarily know the difference between a gerund and a gerundive (in fact, it is disputable whether gerundives exist in English), but you should have a pretty good idea of the difference between a gerund and a participle. For those who are not sure of the difference, a gerund is a noun formed from a verb (as in "Walking is good for you,") while a participle *looks* the same, but functions as an adjective ("Walking down the street, the boy was whistling.") Understanding the rules of grammar will help you understand why some constructions look "funny," and others do not.

The second important point is that the copy editor is *not* hired to re-write the book (unless the book is really bad!). The second worst experience I ever had with a copy editor was with a woman who kept slipping her own bright ideas in among my writing. For example, in a section on portrait photography (it was a photography book), she decided to add a section on pets. The sentence, "When you are photographing people, do not forget the possibility of photographing their pets," I *might* have tolerated. But the following sentence, "Think of all the famous portrait painters of the past who made their name painting animals," was sheer rubbish. I've been thinking for years now, and I still can't think of any! She was also Jewish, and she added a section on Bar Mitzvahs to my (alphabetically arranged!) section on Weddings.

A *good* copy editor would never have stuck in extra material like this. She would have made a note: "Page 76 para 3 — is it worth mentioning the possibilities of photographing pets? Many owners like to have good pictures of their favorite animals," or "Page 95 — list of events to photograph. Should you include Bar Mitzvahs?" Then, I might well have thanked her, and made the change.

And she was only the **second** worst. The worst? Well, without naming names, he was an Austrian who thought that his English was better than mine, which was "too flowery" and "not suitable for an American audience." When he had finished butchering it, I told him that ungrammatical slop like that was not going to appear with my name on it. He wouldn't change the editing, so it appeared under a pseudonym.

Whenever you criticize an author's work, do it gently. Very few writers object to politely-phrased questions, or to suggested corrections; but if you just scrawl "Meaning?" in the margin, or use the blue pencil to cross out sections and make changes, instead of making suggestions, you *will* antagonize the author. On the other hand, I have worked with copy editors who asked very searching questions which actually involved me in a fair amount of re-writing, and I have found them so helpful that I have requested that they be used as copyeditors on my next book, too. This sort of author's recommendation is invaluable to a copy editor, as it means more work next time: publishers much prefer to work with happy, non-combative writers and copy editors, rather than with people who are at loggerheads the whole time.

Unresolved Questions

There can be unresolved questions in both fiction and non-fiction. What happened to a particular character, who had an *affair* with the protagonist and then just faded from view? *Why* is it generally not a good idea to develop your own color film? What is the difference between DIN horsepower, SAE net horsepower, and SAE gross horsepower — and when the author said that a particular car had 255 bhp, which sort of horsepower was he referring to? What did "Bishop" Polk actually do at Chickamauga?

Don't worry. You don't have to know the answers. In fact, it's better if you don't know the answers. That way, the only way you can find out is by asking the author to clarify matters.

When you are doing this part of the job, you are acting (in effect) as a very privileged reader. Most readers, reading a published book, have to put up with what is in there: they can't ask the writer for more information. The copy editor not only *can* ask for more information, it is his or her job to do so.

You need to strike a balance on this, though. It may be that you have a particular interest in a subject and feel that the writer should have put in more about it. You must remember, though, that your job is to resolve only those questions that the writer raised (whether wittingly or unwittingly), and not to raise further questions of your own. At most, you might put in a note which says, "I found this a particularly interesting part of the book, and wonder if it could be expanded."

Lack of Clarity

No writer is ever totally clear at all times. When you are writing something, *you* know what you meant, and it often does not occur to you that someone else might take it differently.

Part of the copy editor's job, though, is to query anything that is unclear. When I am writing, I try to forestall the copy editor on this one by asking my wife to read through the typescript *before* I submit it. Every now and then she will say something like, "What exactly did you mean here?" or "I think I understand this bit, but couldn't you break it up a bit to make it easier to understand?" Often, I'll re-read it, and I won't be able to see the problem until she explains it: "It could mean this or that, and I wasn't sure which." Then, I'll see that it wasn't clear: although I thought I was being clear, I was leaving room for confusion.

A good copy editor will do the same — and just as gently. Once again, I will repeat: be polite to your authors, and they will speak well of you. This translates directly into more work and *more money*.

Inconsistencies

In *Seven Pillars of Wisdom*, T.E. Lawrence was distinctly casual about his spelling of Arab names. For example, "Jeddah" and "Jidda" were used impartially all through the book, and "Bir Waheida" appears also as "Bir Waheidi." His copy editor drew his attention to these, but not very profitably: T.E.'s comment on the second was, "Why not? All one place." And when the copy editor points out that "The Bisaita is also spelled Biseita," T.E. simply replied, "Good."

Fortunately for copy editors, most writers are more helpful about standardizing such matters; but this shows very clearly one kind of inconsistency that a good copyeditor will find.

Another kind of inconsistency is potentially more serious, a straightforward factual error. For example, the most successful V8 engine for the early Ford Mustangs was of 289 cubic inches displacement (cid) and developed 271 bhp. It would not be difficult, though, for a writer to confuse the two figures, either through ignorance or through a typing error. Then, the car suddenly appears with a 271 cubic inch engine and 289 bhp. The copy editor should spot such things, and make a note which says, "Do you mean 271 cid/289 bhp, or 289 cid/271 bhp?

Spelling

There is no help for this one: if you don't spell very well, you are unlikely to be a successful copy editor. Get yourself a good dictionary, and look up any words that look "funny."

One point, though, is that there sometimes are different permitted spellings (such as further and farther), and that English and American spellings are not the same. If you are copyediting the work of an English writer, always check with the publisher whether you are also expected to Americanize it. Usually, you will be: The English are very much more tolerant of American spellings than Americans are of the English spellings.

When you are dealing with direct quotations, you should of course stick to the original spellings: in a quote from English writers, you should therefore leave "colour" and "labour" and "mediaeval," even if you think they are wrong.

Outright errors are another matter. It is common to "tidy up" verbal quotations, but if you leave the mistakes in written or spoken quotations, it is customary to write "(*sic*)" after the mistake. For example, "There ain't no English that can't be verbed (*sic*)."

Grammar

Like spelling, there is nothing to do here but to *learn* the rules. If you never studied grammar at school or at college, you are going to have to check a grammar book out of the library (or even buy it!) and do some studying.

Once again, a word of warning is needed. It is that many "rules" can be broken — in fact, it is disputable whether some "rules" actually exist in English, or whether they are simply inventions based on Latin and Greek. For example, there is no logical reason why you can't split an infinitive in English ("To boldly go..."): the objections simply do not stand up to close scrutiny. On the other hand, unless you already know the rules, you won't know where they are being broken for effect, and where they are just plain wrong. What is more, even if you have no personal objection to split infinitives, there are many people who do not like them; so it is a good idea to use them as little as possible.

Punctuation

Punctuation is fortunately easier to learn than spelling and grammar, at least if you adopt a "functional" approach rather than a "formal" approach.

Functionally, punctuation is a way of conveying the same sense of writing that you would convey in speech. In the last sentence, for example, the comma after the first word is there to reflect the slight pause between "Functionally" and "punctuation." As a rule of thumb, a comma is the shortest break; a semi-colon (;) is a longer break; a colon (:) is longer still; and a period or full stop is the longest break.

In fact, there is a vast amount more to punctuation than that. The "pause" rule will, however, serve very well for nine-tenths of what you read. For the rest, remember that punctuation, like grammar, can be bent to serve the writer's aim. Do not be too keen to impose your view: some writers (myself included) take great care with their punctuation, and do not care to have it altered unless it is plainly wrong, which can of course happen.

"House Style"

"House style" is a matter of consistency and may be applied to spelling, usage, grammar, punctuation, abbreviations, the use of capital letters, and to much else. The "house" in question is, of course, a publishing house, and each publishing house has its own stand on "house style."

Some publishers give their authors (and their editors) thick books, which are effectively manuals of spelling, grammar and general usage. They expect the rules in these books to have the force of law, and to be followed slavishly by all parties, and used in every single book that appears under that publisher's imprint. Other publishers do not seem to care a bit, and still produce books which are every bit as good as the nit-pickers offerings. My own view is that style manuals are "a law to the foolish, and a guide to the wise," and that as long as a book is *internally* consistent, there is no very good reason why it should be consistent with other books from the same publisher. For example, what does it matter whether an author uses "focusing" or "focussing," both of which are permitted spellings, as long as he or she chooses one, and then sticks with it?

The author may or may not pay much attention to the publisher's "house style manual," but the copy editor enjoys no such freedom. On the bright side, style manuals can make the copy editor's life easier: the best of them will answer any questions you may have on grammar and usage. On the down side, they will *only* make it easier if there are not too many changes to the author's text. If the author's style diverges regularly from the style manual, the copy editor should bring this to the attention of the commissioning editor (the person at the publishing house who is in charge of the book), and ask what is to be done. A good editor will then contact the author or put the author and copyeditor directly in touch with one another.

Copyediting on Disk

Although it is not yet widespread practice, an increasing number of publishers like their authors to submit not only a printed copy of their work, but also the original computer disk on which it was written: almost all professional non-fiction writers use word processors now.

Copyediting is then done on the print-out (from which it is transferred to disk) *and on the disk itself.* The "on-disk" copyediting can be done in part by a computerized spell-check system, which automatically spots many typing mistakes or spelling errors, and which can also be set to enforce "house style" spelling such as "focusing" instead of "focussing." If you have an IBM-compatible computer with both 5.25 and 3.5 inch drives (overwhelmingly the standard), you may be able to pick up this sort of work, and very welcome you may be. ALWAYS work on a duplicate disk, though, and back up your own work!

Another Electronic Swindle

I have already referred to the Great Thesaurus Swindle in Section 4.6. Most modern thesauruses are electronic, and another great electronic swindle (from the point of view of a professional writer) is the so-called "Writers' Assistance" programs which are supposed to improve your writing. Needless to say, they don't. If you can't write to begin with, the best of them may be able to turn your text into something along the lines of an acceptable, bland business report; but they can't improve the writing of someone who *does* know what he is doing, and who *does* take pride in it. If a copyeditor ever ran my work through one of these electronic mangles, I would be strongly tempted to commit homicide.

9.2   PROOF READING

Once the manuscript has been copyedited (and checked by the author), it goes to the typesetter. There, it is "keyed in" to be "set" as type.

Clearly, there are many opportunities for problems here. The person who keys in the manuscript is effectively a very fast copy-typist, and even the finest copy-typists make errors. I once had a secretary who almost never made mistakes, but when she did — wow! In a book for an automobile launch, she only made three errors. One was that "the world's strongest body-shell" came out as "the world's strangest body shell;" the second was that a leading competitor was referred to as a Ford Grandad, rather than a Ford Granada; and finally, she referred to the salesman's material being presented "in a green plastic ringdinger" (I had written "ringbinder.") Mind you, I got my own back. Once — entirely innocently, I swear — I referred to her in a memo as a "secretarty."

Anyway, the proof reader's job is to find these and other mistakes, and to "mark them up" for correction. This can be done at one or both of two stages: galley proofs, and page proofs.

Galley proofs (or just "galleys") are "raw" text in the form in which it is keyed in, while page proofs are (as their name suggests) text already laid out in pages. With page proofs, there are not just the typesetters' errors to be dealt with: there may also be layout errors. Typesetters' errors typically include typing mistakes or "literals," missed lines or even paragraphs, and turning over two pages at once. Layout errors arise from the fact that the galleys are physically cut up and pasted onto boards to create page proofs. Once again, two pages can be turned over as one, and the layout artist's scalpel can also "lose" the odd line here and there.

At the galley stage, errors are relatively cheap to fix, but at page proof stage, they can cost more, because a one-word change may alter the length of a paragraph, which alters the layout of a page, which (in extreme cases) alters the layout of a chapter.

Traditionally, the book was sent both to the author and to the proof-reader at both galley and page proof stages, but with modern computerized type-setting and layout, it is becoming increasingly usual for the author to see the book *only* at page proof stage, though the proof-reader may still see it at both stages.

Setting "Off the Disk"

If the author submitted his or her work on disk (Section 9.1 Copyediting on Disk, above), the typesetter can usually "milk" the disk and set directly from that. This saves a great deal of time and money, for several reasons. First, there is no keying-in expense. Second, there is much less delay: an entire book can be set in a few hours. Third, there are no errors introduced by the typesetter; what the author writes (subject to copyediting) is what is set. If a book is set "off disk," it costs about one-third as much as setting in the conventional manner.

Proof Readers' Marks

Contrary to popular belief, proof readers' marks are *not* fully standardized. For example, the mark for "delete" (as in "delete an unwanted character") is a highly stylized letter "d" — but I have seen it written as "r", apparently under the impression that it was short for "remove," and even as what looks like an "e" (for "eliminate"?).

Within reason, almost *any* mark will be understood, because the typesetter can understand the error as well as the proofreader, once it is drawn to his attention. Also, some of the older proofreaders' marks are no longer relevant, because they refer to errors which were only possible with cold metal typesetting; with hot metal, or with phototypesetting (overwhelmingly the most usual today), upside-down letters such as "n" for "u" are impossible.

One thing you need to know, though is that printers' spacing is still calculated in "ens" and "ems," and an "em" is twice as wide as an "en," for reasons which are obvious when you look at them. A short dash is an "en" in length; a long dash is an "em" in length, and is often represented in a manuscript by two dashes together.

Usually, each correction is indicated by two marks, one in the text and one in the margin. The following two pages contain examples of some typical proofreader's marks.

Message	Marginal Mark	Text Mark	Corrected version
Delete	ℰ	He reads the a book	He reads the book
Close up	⌒	He read the bo͡ok	He read the book
Delete & close up	ℰ̃	He read the boook	He read the book
Change to capital	Cap	he read the book	He read the book
Change to lower-case	lc	He reaD THE BOOK	He read the book
Use lower-case letter	lc	He read The book	He read the book
Reset in italic	ital	Don't do that!	*Don't* do that!
Reset in Roman type	Rom	What *can* it be?	What can it be?
Reset in boldface	bf	The word was nor	The word was **nor**
Reset in small capitals	sc	The sign said Stop	The sign said STOP
Transpose	trs	He the book read	He read the book
Indent one em	☐	Call me Ishmael	Call me Ishmael
Insert period	⊙	He read the book⋀	He read the book.
Insert semi-colon	⎮;	the book⋀then he	the book; then he
Insert colon	⊙	wanted⋀so he watched	wanted: so he watched
Insert letter	o⋀	He read the bok	He read the book
Insert hyphen	/=/	Mr. Wycliffe⋀Jones	Mr. Wycliffe-Jones
Insert one-em dash	/m̄/	had⋀if only because	had — if only because
Insert comma	⋋	Don't⋀please	Don't, please
Insert apostrophe	˅	Dont⋀do that!	Don't do that!
Insert quotation marks	˅ ˅	⋀EUREKA⋀ he said	"Eureka," he said
Insert subscript	⋀₂	Water is HO	Water is H_2O
Insert superscript	²˅	E = MC	E = MC^2

Message	Marginal Mark	Text Mark	Corrected version
Insert question mark	?	What is this~	What is this?
Let it stand	stet (or) st.	He read the book	He read the book
Spell out	sp	to the UN	to the United Nations
Query to author	(?)	if youanls can	[seeks clarification — you? you-all? you scan?]
Paragraph break	¶	ends.[Start new	[start new paragraph from mark]
No paragraph break	no ¶	ends.⌐Start new	[do not start new paragraph]
Align type	align //		[normally refers to shaky paste-up]
Move left	⌐		
Move right	⌐		These are
Move up (raise)	⊓		self-explanatory
Move down (lower)	⊔		

The following marks normally apply to cold-metal type only:

Message	Marginal Mark	Text Mark	Corrected version
Broken letter		I aⓍ	I am.
Wrong font	w.f.	Typeface	Typeface
Inverted letter	⊖	Mnst you?	Must you?
Insert leading	ld. ———		["leading" is the space between lines of text]
Straighten type	═══		[May also apply to paste-ups]

You also need to know that type which is underlined in the manuscript should be set in italic in the book; it's just an easy way of distinguishing between Roman type (the regular variety) and italic.

9.3 INDEXING

There are few things more infuriating than knowing something is in a book, but being unable to find it. Even T.E. Lawrence provided a substantial synopsis at the beginning of *Seven Pillars*, despite his statement that "half-way through the labor of an indexing to this book I recalled the practice of my ten years' study of history; and realized that I had never used the index of a book fit to read."

Most of us are more tolerant of indexes, and a good index can make a reference work still more useful, even if it is not "fit to read." Often, a writer will create his or her own indices, but there are still many occasions where the publisher prefers to hire a professional indexer: the writer may be out of the country, or incompetent, or not interested, or the book may have been an outright sale, and indexing wasn't in the contract. One way or another, there are plenty of opportunities for professional indexers.

Choosing the Index Entries

Indexing is not difficult, but it does require application, perseverance, and a tidy mind. The easiest way to do it is with a photocopy of the page proofs and a "highlighter" pen. You then begin by highlighting all the topics that you think it would be useful to have in the index. In this paragraph, for example, you might highlight "page proofs," "highlighter," and "index." That way, anyone who looked in the Index would find those three "key words" that would lead them to this paragraph.

In choosing the topic to highlight, though, you need to be careful. Too many references, and the index becomes unwieldy. You certainly would not want to highlight "paragraph," and you probably would not want to highlight "typeset." Too few references, and the index is insufficiently comprehensive. What I normally do is highlight more than I expect to put in the index, and then when I am compiling the index, I omit the references that seem unnecessary.

Making the Index

There are two easy ways to make an index. One is with file cards, on which you write each topic that you want in the index, and put the page number alongside; as the same topic is repeated, you just add more page numbers to the same topic. You end up with an inconvenient stack of index cards, in alphabetical order, of course, but all you need to do at the end is to copy-type the entries on the cards to create the index.

Even easier is indexing with a computer. Instead of file cards, you enter the topics and page references on a computer, inserting more as need be. Some programs even have "alphabetizers," to make sure that your index really is in alphabetical order (it is quite easy to make mistakes when you are tired). Then, you just print out the completed index at the end.

There are also several difficult ways to make an index, but they involve lots of crossing-out and copying, so they are not worth going into here!

9.4   "BLURB" WRITING

"Blurb" writing definitely offers the fewest opportunities of any of the jobs outlined in this chapter, and it requires a special skill — which I know I haven't got, and which you may not have either — to write those little summaries of books which appear on the dust-jacket or the back cover, and sum up the book in magically few words.

If you *can* do it, though, it is surprisingly well paid, and there is a lot of work about. A really good "blurb" is one of the strongest selling tools a book can have, and publishers are willing to pay hundreds of dollars to "blurb" writers who can pick out the salient points of a book, weld them together into a coherent whole, and then make that whole sound like the sort of book that you would really want to read.

In order to write a first-class "blurb," you need to read the whole book, and you need to read it fast enough to ensure that you have a "picture" of the book in your mind when you start writing: this is not a job for slow readers! The next book you read, try writing a "blurb," and see how you feel about it. Check the length of "blurbs" on books you already own, or books in the library (a typical length is 50-150 words, and short "blurbs" are generally more effective). Model your style on the *best* of these. After you have written ten or twenty "blurbs," compare your earliest efforts with your latest ones, and see whether this really is a field for you. As I've already said, it's a skill that I don't possess, so it's not a subject on which I can give you specific advice. As an earlier edition of this book put it, "You'll need to be aggressive, persuasive, witty and lovable all at once."

10.0 <u>MARKETING AND REVIEWING</u>

Once again, this is a short chapter. Freelance book marketing is a field with limited opportunities, and it is not really the sort of business that you can do without making a major commitment of time, energy and resources. There are more opportunities in reviewing, but the competition is fierce and the financial rewards are not very high.

Having said this, the rewards of book marketing can be very good indeed — it's a high-profile publicity business — and when it comes to book reviewing, most of us would find no fault with a job that pays us (albeit modestly) to do what we would be doing anyway, namely reading books, *and* provides us with free books and the thrill of seeing our names in print!

10.1 <u>BOOK MARKETING</u>

The concept of book marketing is comparatively new: it is only in the last ten or twenty years that the book publishers have done much more than leave their newly-published books to sink or swim, with no more marketing support than an advertisement in *Publisher's Weekly* or *The Bookseller* and maybe an author tour.

Today, there are many more books being published, and there are more people in publishing who have heard of marketing. The result is that some books are quite intensively marketed. In other words, the publisher makes a real effort to ensure that people actually know about the book.

Where do you come into this? Well, there are several ways. An expert publicist — which you could quite easily become, given a little practice — will either create or put together the whole package given below, but until you become expert, you may be happier just doing a part of the job.

The great thing about being a book publicist is that all you need is the right personality. There are some book publicists who can get people to review the most boring books, or to come along to the most unlikely launch parties, *purely* because the publicist has a reputation for being fun. Journalists will actually say, "The book looks like rubbish, but Joanne's parties are always fun — I'll go." Being able to engender that sort of attitude in people is worth big bucks to a publisher!

Press Kits

A press kit is a background information pack which supplements, or in some cases even replaces, a review copy. It normally consists of a folder, which may either be a publisher's "generic" folder (with the company logo, etc.) or a specially-printed folder to promote a particular book. Inside, there is a press release, to which I shall return in a moment. Then, there may be pictures from the book (if it is illustrated), and possibly a picture of the author.

The press release has to meet several conflicting requirements. It has to be brief, or the recipient will not bother to read it. It also has to contain all the information that the publisher wants to convey. It must be positive (no one wants to run down their own product), but it must not be mere empty puffery: it has to *say* something. It must also be written in a way that the recipient can "lift" word-for-word, if need be. Although some editors prefer to read the book (or to give it to a reviewer — see Section 10.2, below), others are quite happy to use press releases with little or no rewriting. If they are overworked, or just lazy, a well-written, ready-to-use press release makes life easier for them!

Meeting these conflicting requirements is not easy. One of the easiest ways to do it is to use two or three pieces of paper, each with about 100-150 words. The first one is a (favorable!) review, along the lines described in Section 10.2. The second sheet goes a little deeper: some information about the writer, and past or forthcoming books. The third (if appropriate) is local: PROMINENT AUTHOR VISITS BAKERSFIELD (or wherever), with information about forthcoming appearances; there will of course be separate invitations to any parties, press conferences, or whatever. A really brilliant publicist would be able to write the three sheets so that all three could be used in sequence, so as to make a single massive article, but that would require remarkable skill.

Each separate sheet will be written in what publicists call "descending triangles." This means that the most important part of the release will be as early as possible, with the least important stuff at the end. The reason for this structure is that most editors cut from the bottom, so you put information that you can best afford to lose at the bottom of the press release.

Press Mailing

Obviously, a press pack has to be sent out to the press. Who compiles the press mailing list, and actually sends out the goodies? Well, it may be someone that the publisher employs full time, or it may be farmed out to a publicity agency that uses freelance help (that's you again), or it might be given straight to a freelance publicist — you yet again!

To whom do press packs go? Most people immediately think of local newspapers, but there is far more to it than that. There are the local "free sheets," for a start, and then there are local radio and TV stations, to say nothing of specialist and national magazines. A good publicist will be able to compile a list of potential recipients, and send them the press pack. And, of course, once the list is compiled it can be added to, and used again and again.

Launch Parties

Launch parties are fun, but they can also be a double-edged sword. On the one hand, you have the champagne, the dainty food, the rich and famous. On the other, you have drunks and gate-crashers. Many writers live, in Alen Coren's felicitous phrase, "under the shadow of the corkscrew," and I have seen several authors and others as drunk as judges at launch parties.

This may seem like an odd thing to emphasize, and maybe it is; but my reason for emphasizing it is to remind you that if you organize a launch party, you are not there as a guest. Anything that goes wrong is something that you have to sort out. The drunks and the gate-crashers are only one possibility. What if the author fails to turn up? (It happens — regularly.) What if there are not enough review copies for all the guests, or enough press packs? And are there taxis available to take people home?

At the other extreme, a launch party has to be lively enough to be memorable. If it is soggy canapes, cheap and nasty champagne served warm, and boring people, the organizer has failed again (and I've been to more than enough press parties like that!)

If this somewhat bleak picture does not depress you, great: go for it. If you can keep your head when all about you are losing theirs, you'll probably make a great book launch organizer. If on the other hand you are a teetotaller with strong views on alcohol, you won't find many people who want you to organize their launch parties.

Author Tours

An author tour is like a launch party, only more so. You have to schedule the tour; arrange venues; arrange transport and accommodation; and (once again) take care of problems like closed bookstores, unrecorded bookings, lost tickets and addresses, and anguished maiden ladies who run literary groups and didn't expect the author to turn up drunk.

From this, it's clear that you need to be the right sort of person to do this. It might suit someone who had been a PA (personal assistant) to a high-powered businessman, but who left to have children or to build a lifestyle where she (or he) was more in control. It might suit almost anyone with a strong, calm personality and plenty of organizational ability. But if you tend to panic, or if you don't like stress, forget it.

Book Reviewing

Book reviews are a form of advertising, which is why publishers are willing to send out large numbers of copies of books for nothing, in the hope that they will be favorably reviewed — or reviewed at all, for that matter.

In fact, book publishers generally don't mind a bad review. As long as the book is reviewed, people will be informed that it exists. Sometimes, a bad review will prompt people to pick up the book, just to see if it is as bad as the reviewer says. If it isn't (and how many reviewers would you trust?), they may buy it anyway.

It is only fair to say, though, that book reviewing is not as easy as it looks, at least if you want to do it well: you can't just say "I liked it" or "I didn't like it." In order to write a good review, you need to have some knowledge of competing books (this is more important with non-fiction that with fiction); you need to be able to write pretty well yourself, because as soon as you start criticizing someone else's work, you inevitably invite criticism yourself. Then again, not all book reviews are well done: the old joke about the small-town paper where the sports editor also does the theater reviews and book reviews is not necessarily all that far from the truth, and you can probably do a better job of reviewing books than some jock who has been drafted from the sports page. The techniques of selling book reviews (or, more accurately, of selling yourself as a book reviewer) are covered in Chapter 12.

The easiest way to write a book review is to approach it from the point of view of the person who is going to read the review. You have read enough reviews: what do you want to know? I suggest that the following things are the most important:

Content

The first thing you want to know when you read a review is what the book is about, and what sort of market it is aimed at. This can be disposed of quite quickly: "a popular history of the Civil War," or "a scholarly biography of Robert E. Lee." That way, you can say later that "this is a popular history, so it does not go into the scholarly controversy of States' Rights," or "for the author of a scholarly book, Mr. _____ seems to have an extremely poor understanding of Lee's opinion of Grant."

Quality of Content

The criteria for quality of content will vary according to whether it is a fiction book or a non-fiction book. In fiction, it is enough that the book should be original and interesting, and that it should not contain any glaring factual errors. After all, even fiction books contain facts, and a book about motorcyclists would elicit howls of derision if it referred to someone changing the chain on a BMW, because all BMWs are shaft-driven. Chapter 4 will give you plenty of ideas on how to judge the content of a fiction book.

In non-fiction, there is more to consider. How comprehensive is the book? How well structured is it? How easy is it to read? Here, the guidelines laid down in Chapter 7 will make it very much easier for you to analyze the book.

Quality of Writing

Once again, Chapters 4 and 7 will help you to judge the quality of a book. In particular, Sections 4.2 and 4.3 are relevant to fiction, and Section 7.3 is useful when it comes to judging the quality of writing in a non-fiction book.

Author

In some cases, it may be relevant to say something about the writer. For example, John Le Carre is well known for his cold-war spy stories, and Bruce Catton's name is synonymous with the Civil War. To review one of their books without referring to the rest of their work would be unusual. Even if an author is not well known, he or she may have special qualifications (or a hidden agenda) which will affect the reader's appreciation of the book. For example, a "New Right" Republican book called "The Kennedy Years: A Reappraisal" would be very different from a book with the same title written by a personal friend of John F. in the 1960s.

Competing Books

Even if a reviewer does not mention competing books by name (which may or may not be appropriate), the review should still be informed by an awareness of what else is available, so that the book under review can be assessed (for example) as "yet another me-too analysis of the Near Eastern situation" or as "an original book with new insights, drawing on unpublished archives concerning the founding of the state of Israel."

Publication Data

Also, of course, you will want to give the title, the name of the author, the name of the publisher, the date of publication, and the price. Don't laugh: *any* of these can be missed out, even the title. Sometimes, the sub-editor will decide to run a "clever" headline instead of the book title, and the title gets lost as a result. If the sub-editor cuts it, that's his problem; but all the information should be there when you send it in. What is more, all that vital information should be at the beginning of the review, not the end. Remember where they cut from!

Other Information

In some newspapers, you may also wish (or be required) to say where the book is available, e.g. "Available from Jones' Bookstore on Main Street, and The Book Nook on Broadway."

If there is any other information that is of interest, you should also include it: for example, if the author will be signing books at Jones' on Tuesday, *say so*.

10.2   REVIEW CLIPPING

Some publishers, some agents, and even some authors, retain clipping services to collect reviews of their books. Once they have the clippings, though, what do they do with them? If they have any sense, they photocopy them, put the original in their files, and give the photocopy to a publicity agent. The publicity agent then uses them to create more promotional material. This may seem like a minor part of the job, but it can be an important one. After all, if you have all the publicity material; if you know the author personally, and his or her likes and dislikes — well, you are the most likely person to be given the next publicity assignment, aren't you?

11.0 <u>ACQUIRING AND HONING SKILLS</u>

You can divide the skills that I have described in this book into three groups. There are the ones you already have; the ones you don't need; and the ones you don't have —*yet*.

You probably have a good idea already of the skills that you do have. As I said at the beginning of the book, you are almost certainly better educated than most of the people you know. Whether your formal education is extensive or not, you have refined and polished it by your reading. Of course, if you don't already read books for pleasure, there is not much likelihood of your successfully reading them for profit!

What do I mean, though, by "the skills you don't need"? Don't you need *all* the skills that are described in this book, in order to be successful?

No, you don't. As I have said repeatedly, there are all kinds of opportunities in all kinds of fields. Some of these fields will attract you. Others may well leave you cold. There may also be a third group, where the job that is described *sounds* attractive, but you know that really, you wouldn't want to do it. Take the question of marketing and publicity, described in the last chapter. Most of us like the idea of going to launch parties, but we don't like the idea enough to make the effort to organize them. For someone else, that information might be invaluable; for others, it will be a complete waste of time.

Or alternatively, the idea of being a book publicist may have fired your imagination: you would much rather do that, instead of earning a quiet, steady, and possibly quite handsome income as a freelance copyeditor. You accept that stress and aggravation is a part of the job; you regard that as a small price to pay for the interest and excitement, the chance to meet writers and publishers and others on equal terms, and the opportunities to earn a *lot* of money if you can build a successful public relations and marketing company. That's good, too. But you won't need to learn proofreaders' marks, and the whole of Section 8.1 (Artwork and Illustration) will be irrelevant as far as you are concerned. This is a book of opportunities, not a text book where you have to work through every example.

OK: so much for the skills you already have, and the skills you don't need. Now for the skills that are either lacking completely, or that need to be polished up before you are happy with them. You can't really separate the process of acquiring and honing skills, so we'll look at the two processes together. There are three main ways to acquire and hone skills. They are practice, books, and courses.

11.1   <u>PRACTICE</u>

With any kind of literary endeavor — and regardless of what you may think, most of what is in this book is concerned with literary endeavor — the most useful single thing that you can do is to *practice*.

Many people do not realize this. Either they are obsessed with the belief that they have to learn from an EXPERT, or they study things as a way to escape from actually doing them.

This is illustrated by a lovely story about (I believe) Dylan Thomas. He was invited to address a group of would-be writers. The word spread that the Great Man was coming, and on the appointed day, he had a lecture-hall full of wannabee writers. He strode into the hall and up to the lectern; seized it; and said majestically,

"How many of you want to be *writers*?" (You have to imagine the rich, Welsh emphasis on *writers*.)

They all nodded, raised their hands, and muttered, "I do."

He looked around him; he could see that enthusiasm ran high. Then he let them have it.

"Right," he said, "why the **** aren't you home writing?"

The same is true of reading. When it comes to reading books, you already have been "home reading." What you probably have *not* been doing, though, is trying to analyze the books that you have read, clearly and concisely, as if you were doing so for other people.

Book Analysis

Chapters 4 and 5 will help you to analyze fiction; Chapter 7 is intended to help you analyze non-fiction. What we are concerned with here is with choosing the books to analyze, and with practicing analysis.

Choosing books — It is a good idea to begin by going to your library and checking out three books. The first should be the kind of book you read frequently, just for fun; in my case, science fiction, or books on photography. The second is a book on a subject that you have a slight interest in, or where you already have a small amount of knowledge; for me, maybe shooting, or a historical novel. The third is a book where you are completely at sea; again, I might choose a book on computer repair or a cowboy novel.

Read each of them in turn (or all at once, if that's how you normally read). As you read, make notes on the books, using the headings in Chapters 4, 5 and 7 as appropriate.

The reason for choosing three kinds of books like this is to check for yourself the kind of range that you can *really* handle. Repeat this exercise two or three times, or more — it isn't costing you anything, and you are learning a great deal in the process.

Practicing analysis — There is one golden rule here: WRITE IT DOWN. It is all too easy to persuade yourself that you have it "all in your head," so you don't need to write it down. When you are facing the blank sheet of paper, or the blank computer screen, you may be amazed at how little you have in your head — or how much! I'm not being rude: there are times when I *think* I have plenty to say, but when it comes to the crunch, I realize I don't — and I write tens of thousands of words a year, probably hundreds of thousands, because I do it for a living. If I get stuck, I bet you can, too. And then there are other times when the words come pouring out, and I have to cut them down to the requisite numbers.

Be as methodical as you can, and don't be afraid to go back and change things — or to tear up all that you have already written. It is the only way that you will learn how to tame words, and how to make them do what you want.

When you have written your analyses, or reviews, or whatever, re-read them, and then make any corrections that are needed. Then set them aside for a while: anything from a few days to a few weeks. Come back to them, and look at them anew. This re-reading is essential for developing an awareness of your own strengths and weaknesses. Are you logical? Do you say all that needs to be said? Is the emphasis where you want it? At first, this can mean painful re-writing, but later it will become second nature to check things while you are writing.

You may also want to show your "reports" or "reviews" or "press releases" to friends, to get their reactions. You know that you are on the right trail when, instead of criticizing your writing, they say "I'd like to read that," or "That sounds awful — how did you manage to finish it?"

Book Reviews

I haven't given any sample reviews in this book, because there are so many different ways that books can be reviewed. What newspapers and magazines do you normally read? Look at their book reviews, particularly in the light of Section 10.2. Count the words: how long is a typical review? Does the reviewer introduce himself or herself, or is the book left to speak for itself? Are there extensive quotes from the book, or none?

Once you can answer these questions, try "reviewing" books in the same way that I suggested analyzing them in the previous section, Book Analysis: a mixture of the familiar, the partly familiar, and the unfamiliar.

"Blurb" Writing

You've guessed it. Apply the same techniques as was described in Section 11.1 and write "blurbs." This is an area where getting someone else's reaction is all but essential: as soon as you have any confidence in your "blurbs," start showing them to other people!

No matter how short and concise your blurbs may be, always see if you can then trim them still further. You need to preserve an easy readability while cutting out every single word that is not absolutely necessary.

Writing Press Releases

Once you have written your "press releases" — on the same plan as outlined in Section 1.1 above — and let them "rest" for a while, try editing them. Just remove the last paragraph to begin with: I'm not joking, that's what a lazy sub-editor will do to make it fit into a space that's a bit too short. Then cut the next-to-last paragraph. Have you lost any essential information yet?

Copyediting

Practicing copyediting is somewhat more difficult than practicing reports, reviews, "blurbs" and press releases. After all, where do you find "raw" manuscripts? One of the easiest answers is at a writers' circle or a writers' conference: there's more about these in the next chapter. Or, of course, if you are already reading manuscripts for a publisher or agent, you can take a photocopy and practice on that — just don't practice on the original! For another possibility, tie up with anyone who uses any kind of printed material, whether press releases or newsletters: a community theater, perhaps, or a local historical society. See Section 9.1 for further information on what a copyeditor does.

Proofreading

Now, life really is interesting. If you can copyedit, you can probably proofread too, but where can you get the material you need? This is one of the few places where you may actually find that a course (Section 11.3 below) is the only easy option.

On the other hand, if you can get access to raw typescripts through a writer's circle or even a community or parish newsletter, you don't need much practice to get good. For that matter, many small, local newspapers are so badly "subbed" (sub-edited, or copyedited and proofread) that you can practice in their columns!

At first, incidentally, you may find that reading the manuscript out loud is a great way to spot problems; it forces you to notice every single word, and stops you "skipping" as most fast readers do. Another technique is to use a small ruler to isolate each line in turn, sliding it down the page.

Indexing

Practicing indexing is dead easy. Go to a thrift store, and buy any non-fiction book with an index. DON'T LOOK AT THE INDEX, except to check that it is there. Read the book, and mark it up and make an index in the way described in Section 9.3. Then, compare your index with the one in the book!

This is not an exciting exercise, but it certainly will tell you (a) whether you are likely to be any good at indexing and (b) whether you are really interested in doing it.

Illustration

Once again, you can practice this by reading a book and then trying to create illustrations that "work." It is more difficult to ignore the illustrations in a book than it is to ignore the index, but don't worry about that: at least at first, it will not do you any harm to be influenced by work that has already been published.

One very specialized area of illustration, which pays very well indeed if you can do it, is cover (and other) illustrations for *fiction* books. Read the book; sleep on it; and see if, in due course, you can both invent and realize an illustration based on the story.

Research

This is possibly the most difficult area of all to practice, and the only approach I can recommend is to set "self assignments," for yourself. Begin with something fairly easy: here are a few suggestions:

- A chronology of the American Civil War, with the main battles in sequence
- Rebuilding an automobile gearbox
- Practical glass-blowing

Once you have a basic understanding of the subject, take another topic which derives from the original idea and is more specialized. For example:

- Treatment of prisoners
- Selection of gear-ratios for racing
- Formulae for colored glasses

See what you can find out about these more specialized subjects. You could even, if you wished, try to get even more specialized — but you will soon run into an interesting phenomenon. It is that there is very little "middle ground" in most types of learning. There are plenty of very general works, and usually quite a lot of highly specialized books, but there is not much in between. For example, books about the Civil War are a dime a dozen (almost literally, if you strike it lucky in the thrift shop), and there are books on individual prison camps. There may even be books on Union camps as a whole, and Confederate camps as a whole. But as far as I know (I haven't checked closely), there is nothing dealing with prisoners of war *on both sides*.

The Parish Magazine and the Community Theater

I have already mentioned parish magazines and the like, and in fact these can be very useful. They are *always* short of help, and if you offer to proof-read or copyedit their material, or to help the local parish historian to research something, they may well be very grateful indeed. You won't get paid anything (not in this life, anyway), but you can gain invaluable experience. The same is true of working with your local community theater: no money, but bags of experience. You can even practice publicity techniques here, writing press releases and running parties. They will be delighted to have someone to help. Consider this route seriously!

11.2 BOOKS

If you need to know more about something, why not read a book on it? Seriously, your friendly neighborhood library (or at least, the one in the nearest half-way reasonably sized city) can almost certainly help you to find out more about almost anything. If you have a clear idea of the subject you want to learn about (such as "Indexing" or "Literary criticism") then the reference librarians should be more than willing to help you.

Of course, one thing you probably *won't* find is anything like this title — "How to Make Money Reading Books" — because making money isn't a "respectable" subject, unless you do it without working by means of investment and stock-market manipulation. This doesn't really matter, though. After all, you already *have* this book! When it comes to the details, though, you'd be astonished at the material that is available for the asking.

There's not much point in saying more about books, because from here on in, books had better be your stock in trade. Think of it as a research project, one to be carried out with the help of your friendly neighborhood reference librarian!

11.3 COURSES

It may seem strange that I have left this one until last, when it is the normal way for everyone to learn everything today: "Oh, yeah, I went to a course," or "I've done a course on it."

There are, however, two good reasons for leaving courses to the last. One is that courses require a significant investment of time and money, and I feel that a book like this should include as many ways as possible to save both time and money. The other is that almost certainly, you won't *need* a course until you already understand a subject pretty well — from this book, from practice, and (if necessary) from books borrowed from your library. Let's look at this second point in more detail.

Selecting Courses

Think of a subject you *don't* know anything about. I can think of lots: taxidermy, knitting, integrated circuit design...you can probably think of a similar list for yourself.

How would you choose a course on any of these subjects? You could not even be sure that it would begin at the right level, and you certainly could not be sure that it would teach you what you want to know. You don't even know whether you would be interested. And for sure, you wouldn't know where was the best place to look to find the right course.

Until you know a good bit about the subjects in question, there is very little point in taking a course — and as you study the subject, you will find out where the courses are. For example, the USDA offers indexing courses, improbably enough. I have no doubt that they are very good: Uncle Sam is very good at this sort of thing. But do you actually want to be a full-time, super-specialized indexer? If not, the information in this book, and a look at a publisher's style manual, will probably tell you all that you need to know about indexing — for example, the fact that McIntosh and McKeown are normally indexed as if they began with "Mac" instead of Mc.

With this in mind, *wait* before you even consider a course. When you are absolutely sure you need one (which may never happen), remember that your local university, community college, or adult education program may well offer what you need as well as all kinds of other useful courses; and so often, your friendly local library is usually the best place to find out.

12.0 <u>MARKETING YOURSELF</u>

As I have repeatedly said, this book is not a "get rich quick" scheme. Sure, I could promise you the moon — but I think you would prefer me to be realistic. If you master the skills that I have described, and if you make a real effort to market those skills to the right people, you *will* earn money. You have already seen that you can take your choice from a wide range of skills, and that those skills are not impossible to acquire.

You also know, from past experience, that "get rich quick" schemes don't work. Of course, you can always win a lottery, or rob a bank; or a rich uncle might die and leave you a million. But in the real world, if you want an honest income, you are going to have to work for it.

It is clear, I hope, that there are many opportunities for freelances in the publishing business; perhaps more than there are in any other major industry. The things to look at now is how to exploit these opportunities.

<u>Don't Tell Anyone About This Book</u>

Imagine that you have spent years in the publishing business. The information in this book is totally familiar to you. Now, someone comes along saying that they have read *one book*, and that they want to work in the same business.

It is only human nature to be dismissive. "I've been doing this for ten years, and you're telling me that you've read one book, and you know all about the business?" They won't take you seriously. So keep quiet about this book. If publishers or agents ask you where you learned all the information in it, be evasive: "Oh, you know, reading, talking to people."

This may sound like strange advice, but it is sound. The information in here is the fruit of many years of working in and around the publishing business. The trouble is, most people "in the business" do not believe that you could possibly learn very much from a book like this. They are wrong, of course; you have seen that for yourself. The danger is, though, that if you tell them that you bought this book, they will lump you in with the "get rich quick" brigade, and refuse to hire you.

This is because they regularly get letters from people who say, in effect, "Dear Sir, I have just bought this book about reading books for money, and it says..."

People who write letters like that have missed the entire point of this book. The editors and publishers and agents that you will be dealing with *do not care* that you have read any books on anything. What they care about is that you can do the job that they need done, whether it is acting as a paid reader, or a copyeditor, or anything else. If you can persuade them that you can do the job, then *they will hire you*. It's as simple as that.

As I say, this does not mean that this book is useless, or anything to be ashamed of. Far from it. This is the book that gives you the behind-the-scenes information, the inside track that you need to succeed. Without this book, you might never have a chance of breaking into this lucrative and interesting field. But the information it contains is effectively taken for granted by the people who are going to hire you. They already know it. It is the fact that *you know it too* that means you can work with them. That's all that matters to either of you!

Check *Literary Market Place*

LITERARY MARKET PLACE, normally abbreviated to LMP, is the "bible" of the American publishing industry. The vast majority of agents and book publishers are listed in it, with names, addresses, and other useful information. It is published annually, and is very expensive, but almost all libraries keep it.

Use LMP to get the names of agents and publishers, and also to see what *sort* of work they do. There is no sense, for example, in offering to read fiction manuscripts if the agent or publisher in question handles only non-fiction, and vice versa. One agent I spoke to in the course of checking facts for this chapter told me that his entry in

LMP says clearly that he handles only non-fiction; but eight to ten per cent of the queries he receives deal with fiction.

Writer's Market

As it's name suggests, *Writer's Market* is a publication for writers. Sometimes derided as the "poor man's LMP," it fills a different need, contains some information that LMP does not, and is a lot cheaper. Like LMP, it is another annual, and although many of its buyers are clearly the worst kind of wannabee, you should not write it off because of that. I don't buy it every year, but I buy it most years.

12.1   THE FREELANCE LIFE

Often, I have earned over a thousand dollars in a single week — sometimes well over a thousand dollars — just by sitting here at my desk, tapping one-fingered on the keyboard of my computer; the few people who have seen me work agree that I must be the world's fastest one-fingered typist, but I am strictly one-fingered. I don't have a degree in English; I haven't formally studied the subject since I was about sixteen, which is about a quarter of a century ago as I write this. When I finish this book, I'm going to get into my new car, which I paid cash for (admittedly, it's a very modest car), and I'm going to go up to Northern California for a long weekend. I don't know how long yet: maybe only three days, maybe as much as five, because it depends on how I feel. Sounds like a pretty good lifestyle, hey?

That's why I like freelance work. I hate getting up in the morning: if I'm out of bed before eight, it's unusual. At the other end of the day, I may be working until midnight; but maybe I'll have taken three or four hours off during the day to go into town or out for a walk, and we have an old-fashioned family dinner where we frequently sit around for an hour and a half or two hours, talking and enjoying our food. Sometimes I can't believe how fortunate I am.

That's because it hasn't always been like this. There have been times when my wife and I scoured the house for returnable bottles, because we needed the dollar or so that we could get from the deposits; when we have gone through the pockets of clothes in the closet, trying to find a few coins.

I am, therefore, better qualified than most people to talk about the advantages and pitfalls of working as a freelance. I've been doing it for about a decade, and I know that it takes a while to succeed. I also know that when success comes, it can sneak up on you without your really being aware of it: you are still working the same way that you have always done, but suddenly, you have some money in the bank and you can have a bottle of wine with your dinner.

Don't Burn Your Bridges

If you are reading this, there is a good chance that you fall into one of three categories. You already have a job, but you could do with some extra money (couldn't we all?). Or you are at home, perhaps with children, and you need a way that you can earn money without leaving home. Or maybe you are unemployed — maybe recently laid off — and you are exploring all the avenues that are open to you.

In all three cases, there is one piece of advice that applies. Don't put all your eggs in one basket. At first, the freelance road is bumpy and uneven: there will be times when you earn, and times when you don't. You may earn $10,000 in a couple of months — and then nothing at all for another three months. It has happened to me! If at all possible, *do not rely* on your income from freelance work in the publishing field until the work has smoothed out to a (reasonably) steady flow, and until you have learned how to budget on the basis of a "boom and bust" income.

Certainly, if you are currently employed, DO NOT quit your regular job until you have a genuine, reliable, steady income from freelance work — and remember that as long as you have both a regular job and freelance income, you effectively have two jobs. Once you give up your regular job, you will need to replace the lost income with more freelance work. When I quit my last full-time job, many years ago, I was earning about $10,000 or $12,000 a year (I've forgotten, quite honestly!), and I felt the chill when that monthly paycheck dried up!

You may also wish to explore other avenues of freelance work as well as publishing — though quite honestly, there is so much choice in publishing, and so much work around, that there is no very great need. Even so, you may wish to look at some of the other titles in the Broughton Hall list.

And Now the Good News

The reason that I feel the need to discourage you from being too enthusiastic about freelance work in the publishing industry is simple. It is that there is *so much* work around that you may decide prematurely that this is all you need to do. You are probably right. But to be on the safe side, give it a few months, or even a year, before you make this your career. That's all; that's my last warning.

12.2 START OUT SMALL

When you first start as a freelance, you have two strikes against you. In the first place, you don't have much experience. In the second place, no one has heard of you.

The lack of experience means that everything takes longer than it would take someone who was more experienced, and that you are not quite as good at the job. This obviously keeps you out of the major league when it comes to earnings.

The fact that no one has heard of you is another factor which decreases the amount you can earn. Understandably, people are always more willing to hire someone with a track record, rather than an unknown, and they will also pay them more. How, then, do you acquire experience and a reputation?

Working for Nothing

If your only interest is in reading, no problem. You can practice using books from the library, and when you are confident that you are good enough, you start hitting the publishers and agents. But if you want to get *editorial* freelance work, you may do well to start out working for nothing.

You should never try to sell anything on price alone. People are too used to the idea that you get what you pay for, and as the old saying goes, "If you pay peanuts, you get monkeys." Either charge a fair rate, or work for nothing.

Now, there are three good ways to work for nothing. One is to work for a worthy cause that has no money: a charity, a church, or whatever. As I have said elsewhere, parish magazines are permanently short of help, and working for them or something similar can give you invaluable experience *and* help a cause you care about. This is also a great place to gain experience in line drawing.

The second way to work for nothing is to work with someone else who is starting up: a new publisher, a would-be writer. Make it clear that you are working for nothing in order to gain experience, and that they are not getting a top-of-the-line professional. I'll come back to writers later, but when it comes to finding small, struggling publishers, go along to any local fair and see what books are *on sale*. The chances are that they will be of local interest, by local publishers. Write to them and explain what you are doing, and why.

The third way to work for nothing is to proofread (or index, or whatever) material which otherwise would receive no professional attention at all. Go along to your local copy-shops or jobbing printers and explain to them what you are doing: they will have brochures and reports which their clients may be pleased to have proofread by an independent person. Put up a notice in your local community college or university, offering proofreading and copyediting. There will be theses, essays and teaching material on which you can practice your skills.

Expanding Your Base

Once you have a few jobs under your belt, three things will happen. First, you will get faster and better at your work. Second, you will get an idea of how long it takes to do things, and of what you have to charge. Third — and this is the magic one — you will find people who need your services.

This is a bit like what happens when you buy a new car. Suddenly, you see all the other similar cars on the road — cars you had never noticed before. You have become "sensitized" to that brand and model. Likewise, when you have done a bit of copyediting, or proofreading, or whatever, you will notice opportunities that you never noticed before.

And, of course, it feeds upon itself. One editor gives you the name of another, or recommends your name to someone else. Before you know it, you're a professional.

12.3   WORKING WITH WRITERS

As I have said elsewhere, the big problem with writers lies in finding a writer with any money. At first, though, you don't necessarily want money. You want manuscripts that you can practice on. Preferably you want published writers, because they can be your introduction to publishers; but that can come later too.

Writers' Groups

The number of "wannabee" writers in the United States is astonishing. I live in central California, a long way from either Los Angeles or San Francisco, and within a hundred miles' radius there are at least half a dozen "writers' circles." In the two big cities, they are probably even thicker on the ground. For the most part, the people who attend these circles or groups are no-hopers: they can't tell a story, they can't write, and they are permanently paranoid about people "stealing their ideas."

For all that they are literary no-hopers, many of them are nice people. Also, there are *some* (precious few!) who have some talent. If you attend a couple of meetings of writers' circles, you will soon learn who they are: the custom is that people read out a chapter or so of their latest work, which is then criticized by all present.

Clearly, these people can supply all the material you need for reading, copyediting, proofreading, and even (if there are any non-fiction writers) indexing. To find out where these circles meet, look in the "what's on" section of your local newspaper, or listen to your local public service radio station, or look for a bulletin board in your local independent bookshop (the chains don't normally have bulletin boards). At this stage, you are almost certainly working for free — though if there are any published authors there (there used to be precisely two, out of a dozen members, at one circle I used to visit from time to time), you may be able to pick up some low-paid indexing or even research work.

Writers' Conferences

A writers' conference is a writers' circle writ large. Normally, the speakers are minor writers and journalists, but at least they have had a few books or some magazine articles published; the wannabees pay good money to listen to their words of wisdom.

I would not recommend paying good money to go to a writers' conference (sometimes called a "Writers' Workshop" instead), but if you can get in for free, that is another matter.

If you are just starting out, and don't yet have a track record, write to the organizers of a few local workshops (they are advertised in the two writers' magazines, *The Writer* and *Writer's Digest*, both of which should be in most libraries) and explain the field that you are in. Offer to copyedit or proofread or criticize selected manuscripts for nothing. They may well take you up. If they do, you are up and running — and because you are "faculty" rather than "student," you may have useful opportunities to talk with the other speakers.

If you *do* have a track record, of course, you may well be able to speak at the writer's conference, and get paid for it. You can speak on any one of a dozen or more topics, such as "preparing a manuscript" or "common flaws in characterization" or "getting your facts right in fiction" or any other topic *drawn from your personal experience*. And, of course, you'll be right in the middle of things for finding more work!

12.4   WORKING AS AN AGENTS' OR PUBLISHERS' READER

To listen to some people, you would get the impression that agents have completely taken over the publishers' functions when it comes to weeding through the "slush pile" (Section 2.2). In fact, it varies widely. Some publishers refuse to look at *any* unsolicited manuscripts; some *say* they refuse to look at them, but take a look anyway; and some plough through them in the old-fashioned way, or send them out to readers.

Agents function in much the same way. The only way to get work as a reader with either a publisher or an agent is to send a *brief* query letter. *Don't* give them a hard-luck story about how you need the money, or any other irrelevant information. You are offering them a business deal, so be businesslike. With the letter, enclose a one-sided resume which shows your particular areas of expertise; obviously, stress those qualities and experiences which will be relevant to the kind of work you are talking about.

To find out which agents and publishers to write to, go through *Literary Market Place* or *Writer's Market*.

Query Letter

One of the best ways to make sure that your query letter is actually read, instead of being consigned to the "circular file" (the waste basket), is to get a name to write to. Either use a trade directory such as *Literary Market Place*, or just telephone the reception desk and say something like, "I wonder if you could tell me the name of the person who deals with hiring readers? I'm just writing a letter, and I need to know whose attention I should mark it for." Once you have the name, write something like this:

```
Dear Mr. Smith [or Ms. Jones, or whomever],

     I understand that you sometimes use freelance
readers. While I realize that there may be nothing
available at present, I would be grateful if you
would place this letter and the accompanying
resume on file.

     The resume gives a good idea of my
background, but it is worth adding that my main
reading interests are not in "literary" fiction; I
am particularly fond of spy stories and westerns,
and after reading literally thousands of such
books over the years, I think I have a pretty good
idea of what appeals to the typical reader of such
books.

     If you would like to see them, I could send a
couple of sample reports based on already-
published books; or, of course, I would be more
than happy to write a report on a sample
manuscript, if you would care to send one.

Yours sincerely,


[Your Name]
```

Notice that the first paragraph is brief and businesslike; the second stresses your particular skills and interests; and the third makes a straightforward offer. If the recipient is interested, he can come back to you; if not — there are plenty of other fish in the sea.

Type the letter on good-quality paper: this greatly increases the likelihood of its being read. The worst thing of all is a hand-written letter on cheap, lined paper torn from a pad or notebook: the only reason that most publishers or agents will read these is for laughs, before throwing them into the bin unanswered.

Some people believe in enclosing stamped, self-addressed envelopes with letters like this. I don't. This is a business deal. If the other person is interested, they will not begrudge the price of a stamp.

Resume

A modern resume or *curriculum vitae* is short and to the point: people no longer want long-winded assurances that you are married with 2.3 children and support the Elks. You normally begin with your name and address; describe your academic qualifications, beginning with the highest and working backwards; run through your employment history, again beginning with your current or most recent job and working backwards, emphasizing those aspects of the job which are most relevant to the work you want to do; write a one-paragraph "pitch" about yourself; and close either with the names and addresses of people who are willing to furnish references (ask them first!) or with the simple statement, "References Available." A sample resume appears on the following page.

Of course, if you think that your present employers might object to your taking part-time work, don't use them as a reference!

Remember too that the person reading your resume does not care how *clever* you are; he (or she) cares how *good* you are at the job that you are proposing to do. People who try to sound clever will often fall flat on their faces by being too "high-falutin'". This does not mean that you have to be aggressively illiterate: it just means that you have to use plain, simple language to describe your talents, instead of indulging in overblown prose in an attempt to disguise the fact that you don't know what you are talking about. I hope that much of this book will serve as a model for such writing.

12.5   WORKING AS A "SCOUT"

A non-fiction "scout" (Section 2.2) generally needs specialist knowledge — but if you have that knowledge, whether it is in

---

JOHN SMITH
123 Lake Road, Anytown CA 94321
Telephone (212) 555-1212

EDUCATION: AA Degree in English, Alan Hancock College, Santa Maria, California (1983)
High School Diploma, Anytown High (1980)

WORK EXPERIENCE: Clerk, Anytown IRS Service Center 1984-present

Responsibilities: filing, expenses for auditors. Requires a methodical and analytical approach, and an ability to tell true from false!

PERSONAL: Although my degree is in English, my main interest is in travel — both armchair and for real. In the year between leaving Alan Hancock College and starting work for the IRS, I traveled extensively in the United States and spent three months in Central and South America. I travel much less now, but I still retain a strong interest in other countries and in traveling within the United States.

REFERENCES: Erasmus Jones,
Professor of Comparative Religion,
Anytown College, CA 94322

Artemus O'Brien
Director, IRS Service Center,
Anytown, CA 94322

American history or in cookery, you may be able to sign a deal with a publisher (or even with several publishers) to act as a scout. A fiction scout merely needs to read a lot! In either case, the thing to do is to write a brief letter in which you stress your knowledge of and interest in a particular subject. Likewise, "slant" your resume (Section 12.4 Resume) to emphasize your interests and expertise.

One thing that you cannot do as a scout, though, is to approach the publisher "cold" with a new prospect. At best, the publisher will say "Thank you very much," and not pay you. At worst, your letter will be ignored. The aim is to set up your relationship with the publisher first, and *then* feed in the ideas. Also, you don't approach the writer directly;

you approach the publisher, and let them approach the writer if they think that this is appropriate.

Almost by definition, most of the people you will recommend will not have agents: if they did, their agents would already be pushing their ideas. You are looking, therefore, for local talent — which you might find at writers' circles, in the local newspaper (or other local periodicals), or at local schools and colleges. You may also be looking at material which is published nationally, but for a restricted or limited audience: clubs, special-interest groups, academic papers. Your opportunities are limited only by the range of *your* interests and contacts.

You may also wish to consider "scouting" for overseas publishers, or (if your work takes you overseas) "scouting" in other countries for U.S. publishers. There is surprisingly little contact between the publishers of different nations, despite the Frankfurt Book Fair every year in Germany, and often a book is not "picked up" by an overseas publisher because they have never heard of it!

Query Letter

Dear Mr. Smith,

Do you ever use literary scouts? I live on California's Central Coast *[or wherever you actually live]*, and as in the rest of the United States, a great deal of material is published locally which is never seen nationally. Also, I belong to the Society for Creative Anachronism *[or whatever your interests are]* and I encounter a good deal of material through them.

My formal academic qualifications are limited -- I never finished college, though I have a high school diploma -- but if you take into account my fifteen years of reading and learning since my

formal education ended, I am well read. My
particular interests are in history, especially
the mediaeval period, and in philosophy. I also
read a great deal of fiction, though I realize
that this is unlikely to be of interest to you as
a non-fiction publisher.

If you have any use for a literary scout in
the central California area, I would be grateful
if you would let me know.

Yours sincerely,

[Your Name]

Don't Overdo It

The way to achieve credibility as a scout is to supply *good* leads. Your job is to act as a filter between the publisher and the would-be writer. If you send recommendations of everyone and his dog to the publisher, they will soon cease to take you seriously. If you send just half a dozen recommendations in a year, and they "bite" on four of them, you will be very much more highly regarded!

12.6 EDITORIAL SERVICES

By now, you should have a pretty good idea of the kind of letters that you need to write in order to get work. With editorial services, however, there may be a test before they hire new proofreaders, copyeditors, or whatever. In your letter, stress your willingness to take a test if need be; say something like:

Dear Mr. Smith,

    Do you ever use freelance copyeditors? I have
been gaining experience in copyediting while working with writers at the Anytown Writers' Circle
and with the Quik-On Kopy Shop, to say nothing of
the parish magazine, Ways of St. Gertrude.

    If you have any kind of copyediting test, I
shall be glad to take it; I have been studying the
subject for some time, and I believe that I can
work to professional standards. The enclosed
resume gives some idea of my background; all that
I can add is that I am quick and reliable. I hope
you are interested; I look forward to hearing from
you.

Yours sincerely,

[Your Name]

    Of course, if you already have professional (paid) experience in copy writing, you can mention this in both your letter and your resume!

Don't Overdo It (Part II)

    By all means, say that you can do both copyediting and proofreading. Be wary, though, of saying that you can do copyediting *and* proofreading *and* indexing; and *don't* say that you can do all of those *and* illustration as well. Even if you can do all of those (and there is no reason why you should not master all of them), the person who reads the letter will be suspicious. You know the old saying: "Jack of all trades, master of none."

    If you really do have all of these skills, offer them to different publishers. There are enough of them, Heaven knows! That way, too, you can see which skills are most in demand, and pitch future letters accordingly.

Start Locally

If you live in New York City, there will be a lot of work around, but there will also be a lot of competition. If you live out in the bush somewhere, there will be less competition, but there will be less work. Even so, it is a good idea to approach smaller, local publishers first, for two reasons. First, they are likely to be more willing to hire someone local. Second, it is quicker and easier to deal with someone where you can actually pick up and drop off manuscripts, or where (at least) you can send them by UPS on the next day; from where I live, in central California, even the regular UPS service to Los Angeles and Hollywood is next-day. If you are *really* out in the bush, learn about UPS Second Day Air, which is surprisingly economical and very much quicker than the "U.S. Snail."

To find addresses, use this book, your local Yellow Pages, and business directories at your local library: the reference librarian will normally be pleased to help you.

12.7   PUBLICITY

Although we have listed some publishers and agents in the book, we have not listed any publicity companies. There are two reasons for this. The first is that while we want to give you as much "directory" material as possible, if we listed *every* opportunity, the book would be a foot thick and would have no room for the "inside track" information that makes up the bulk of the text. The other reason is that publicity companies change before your very eyes: growing, amalgamating, splitting, dying. Reading LMP (see Section 12.0 Check *Literary Market Place*) will give you a much better idea of the publicists' scene.

Also, you might care to write directly to local publishers, asking if they want any assistance with their book marketing. I say "assistance" because they are unlikely to be able to afford a full-service publicity agent, but they may well be interested in farming out a portion of their publicity work to freelances — and I don't have to remind you who I mean by that!

The Local Theater Again

In the last chapter, I mentioned the possibilities of gaining experience while working with a local community theater. Of course, if there is a *commercial* theater, you can also work for them for pay!

12.8   BOOK REVIEWS

As with publicity companies, there is no future in trying to list every single opportunity for book reviewers: basically, you are looking at every single periodical in the United States.

As usual, you have to start out small. There is a better chance of working for your local free sheet (or even your local newspaper) at ten or twenty bucks a throw than there is of breaking straight into *The New Yorker*. As you build a file of reviews, you can approach more and more important newspapers, but make no mistakes: it will take *years* to get into the big league at a dollar a word.

Syndicate

There is, however, one way to earn more money from a single column, and that is to syndicate it. That's right: just like the big-name cartoonists in the funny papers, or the "agony aunts" like "Dear Abby" and Ann Landers. Write to a variety of local newspapers and free sheets, saying something like:

```
Dear Sir,

    Would you be interested in locally-oriented
book reviews? I don't mean reviews of local books;
I mean reviews by a person who understands the
mood and feelings of people here in central Iowa
```

[or wherever you are]. All too often, book reviewers
have a New York mentality, or a Los Angeles
mentality, and we just don't think that way around
here.

If you are interested, I can send some sample
reviews *[you need three, at least]* so that you can see my
style. My resume gives a fair idea of my background, but some sample reviews would tell you
more! Either write to me at the above address, or
call me at (605) 555-1212; if I'm not in, my
answering machine will be.

Yours sincerely,

[Your Name]

Note that you don't mention money, and you don't include the
reviews. People will read a short letter, and if they are interested, they
will contact you for more information. If they see a stack of material,
though, they will as likely as not glance at it, then throw it away
immediately.

When they do write back, they may well mention money, and
you will have to use your own judgement on what you charge each
member of the syndicate. Anything less than five dollars is likely to be
taken as a joke, but you may have difficulty getting much more than
fifteen — though you might go as high as twenty-five. Within thirty
miles of where I live, there must be close to a dozen small publications
that would each chip in a few bucks a week, and if you could sign up
with (say) five of them at an average of ten bucks each, that's $50 a
book and a handsome portfolio. Then, you can start approaching the
state-wide publications and the smaller national magazines.

As before, get addresses from your local Yellow Pages, Chamber of Commerce, trade directories and from LMP/Writer's Market. There are people out there who want to hear your opinions, and who will pay you for them; and there are few things more delightful in life than being allowed to stand on your favorite soap-box *and get paid for it.*

ENVOI: ...AND GET PAID FOR IT

The final words of Chapter 12 were, *and get paid for it*. Always remember that this book is about getting paid for something that you like to do. This means that it *isn't* a conventional get-rich-quick book. Rather, it's a book about getting rich more slowly (well, not *too* slowly), but doing it by doing something that you really enjoy. Years ago, I worked with a Swedish consultancy company whose motto was something like this:

Whatever you do, do it excellently. If you don't do it excellently, it won't be fun, and it won't be profitable. And if you aren't in business for fun or profit, what are you in business for?

I hope you will join me in raising an imaginary glass to the following toast:

"Here's to fun *and* profit."

GLOSSARY AND REFERENCE

Unlike most glossaries, this one also contains words that are *not* in the body of the book. This is because there are many terms which can be explained perfectly well in plain English, but which are normally expressed in printers' or publishers' jargon, whether to save time or purely for traditional reasons. If you are around the publishing business, you are likely (sooner or later) to hear many of these terms.

Abbreviations	Any good dictionary will have a list of (reasonably) standard abbreviations, usually at the back. Abbreviations should, however, be spelled out in full if there is the slightest doubt about what they refer to, or if the abbreviation is an unfamiliar one.
Backlist	See LIST.
Biography / Autobiography	Surprisingly, many people do not realize that an *autobiography* has to be written by the subject of the book. Thus, "My Land and My People" is an autobiography of His Holiness the Dali Lama, written by himself, where "Great Ocean" is a biography written by someone else.
Camera-ready Copy	is "camera ready" when the text has been laid out as it will appear in the final book. It is then photographed using a "process camera," and a special large-format camera for graphic-arts use.
Cast Off	"Casting off" is the process of taking a TYPESCRIPT and estimating how long it will be when it is TYPESET.
"Category" Fiction	Another name for "GENRE" FICTION.
Characterization	The process of making the people in a work of fiction (or in a biography, for that matter) "come alive."

Cold Metal	Early printing presses, which have now almost disappeared except for some kinds of fine-art printing and in poor countries, used individual letters which were set in a frame for printing. See also HOT METAL.
Compositor	The compositor is the person who "composes" or sets up the type for a printing press.
Conversion	If a color photograph is run as a black-and-white or HALF TONE, it is said to be a conversion. Some printers are much better at conversions than others, and some pictures are more suited to conversions than others.
Copy	In addition to its usual sense, "copy" also has two other meanings. One is "text" (which is why a COPYEDITOR is called a copyeditor), and the other is CAMERA READY COPY.
Copyeditor	The copyeditor is responsible for making sure that a manuscript is in publishable form: grammatical, correctly spelled, and free of unresolved questions. See Section 9.1.
Copyright	Copyright is literally the right to copy or reproduce a work. It is obviously intended to make sure that books cannot be "pirated" or reproduced by people who simply steal someone else's work. Infringing copyright is a serious crime, with heavy federal penalties.
Design	The "design" stage of the book is when its appearance and layout are being decided. Usually, the author will have a good idea of the design that is intended, and will work appropriately.
Editor	There are many kinds of editor. The top of the tree is the Commissioning Editor or Senior Editor, who works

for a publishing house and guides the book through production. In big publishing houses, a Senior Editor or Commissioning Editor may be responsible for a whole section of the publisher's LIST, and have several junior editors (or just plain "editors") working for him or her. Next down the tree is the COPYEDITOR, and sometimes the PROOFREADER is known as a "sub-editor," though strictly this is a term used in newspaper offices.

Extent

The "extent" of a book is its length in words. The extent of this book is approximately 50,000 words.

Faction

The dictionary definition of "faction" is to do with supporters of one group or another; but it is sometimes used to describe a book which blends fact and FICTION in such a way that they are indistinguishable. "Faction" is often given away by the phrase, "based on a true story." How solidly it is based, and how true the story, will often be for the reader to judge. Pretending that a novel is a true account is an ancient fictional device.

Fiction/non-fiction

It may seem silly to define fiction and non-fiction, but many people do not seem to distinguish clearly between them. Fiction is a made-up story; non-fiction is a true account of something. Of course, there are some books such as FACTION (and some types of show-biz or political memoirs) where the dividing line is hard to draw.

Four-color Printing

A full color picture can be reproduced using only four colors of ink: cyan, magenta, yellow and black. In order to turn a photograph or a piece of artwork into a form that can be printed in this way, it is SCANNED or SEPARATED. If there is four-color printing on both sides of every page, the printing is said to be "Four back four" or "four by four." If it is full-color on one side, and single-color on the other (usually to save money) it is called "four back one" or "four by one."

Galley Proofs

When a book is first TYPESET, the text is in long columns which bear no relationship to the final page layout. In this form, the proofs are known as "galleys."

"Genre" Fiction

Many of us read *types* of books, such as detective novels, historical novels, horror stories, romances, science fiction, spy stories, war stories, westerns, or whatever. Each of these categories is known as "genre" fiction. Sometimes, there may be sub-genres: hospital romances are sub-genre of romances, while gothic horror is a sub-genre of horror.

Half Tones

If a picture has shades of gray in it — a black and white photograph, for example, or a pencil drawing — it must be reproduced by special technical processes. To printers, such pictures are known as "half tones."

Hot Metal

The earliest printing presses used metal type which was set up or "composed" letter by letter. Later, LINOTYPE machines were used; because the metal was melted, then cast in "slugs" for printing, this was known as HOT METAL printing.

Imposed Proofs

Imposed proofs are the pictorial equivalent of PAGE PROOFS: that is, they are pictures laid out in the same way that they will appear on the final page. They may or may not be accompanied by text. See also SCATTER PROOFS.

Keying In

Unless the type is SET OFF DISK, it must be physically copied (using a keyboard) in order to be set. The process of copying — which is little more than glorified copy typing — is known as "keying in."

Layout	Layout is, as its name suggests, the technique of arranging the book — the text and the pictures — as they will appear on the printed page. Rough layouts are sketches; final layouts should be CAMERA READY COPY.
Line Reproduction	Line reproduction is where any illustration is solid ink, like type on a page: there are no shades of gray.
Linotype	"Linotype" is a long-established trade name for a machine that is used for HOT METAL TYPESETTING. The operator uses a keyboard, which *via* a complicated set of linkages sets up molds into which molten metal is run to create "slugs" or lines of type — hence "line-o-type."
List	A publisher's "list" is the books that he publishes. The word is used in several different ways. Big publishers may have several "lists" (different kinds of fiction, different non-fiction subjects, etc.). The "backlist" is book already published, steady sellers that are not allowed to go OUT OF PRINT, and the "Spring List" and "Autumn List" are the books published in the spring and the fall, logically enough; summer and winter lists are less usual. Usage: "This book will be published in the Spring 1992 list."
Manuscript	Strictly, a manuscript should be hand written (it comes from the Latin, meaning "written by hand"), but nowadays it also includes TYPESCRIPTS.
Marking Up	Before a MANUSCRIPT can be TYPESET, it must be "marked up" with instructions to the typesetter: where to set bold type, where to indent, and so forth. This is normally the responsibility of the in-house editor at the publishing house.
Offset Lithography	This is a printing process, the details of which need not concern us here, which allows books to be printed

without using metal type: everything is converted to photographic film. This is overwhelmingly the most usual way to print books and magazines today.

Out Of Print

A book is out of print when it is no longer commercially available new. Some publishers specialize in reprints of out-of-print books, especially if these books are in the PUBLIC DOMAIN.

Page Proofs

After GALLEY PROOFS have been checked, the book is "laid out" in the form in which it will be printed, with the text divided up into pages.

Paste Up

Formerly, GALLEYS were actually cut up with a scalpel and arranged on "boards" to create PAGE PROOFS. For obvious reasons, this was referred to as "paste up." Today, more and more "paste up" is actually done electronically.

Phototypesetting

Originally, all typesetting was done using old-fashioned type or COLD METAL. Then, HOT METAL came in. Now, the vast majority of books are printed from type that is set photographically and reproduced by OFFSET LITHOGRAPHY.

Protagonist

The protagonist (the word comes from the Greek) is the principal character in a book, or (to be more accurate) the main actor in a play.

Public Domain

When a book is not protected by COPYRIGHT, whether because the period of copyright has expired, or because it was never protected (as with some Federal publications), or for any other reason, anyone may reprint it, or quote from it, or do what they will with it, without any problems.

Production

The "production" stage of a book includes editing, typesetting and paste-up; printing and binding may be regarded as a part of production, or as a separate later stage.

Proofreading

A proofreader is responsible for finding mistakes in a typescript or in GALLEY PROOFS and PAGE PROOFS. See Section 9.2.

Scanning

In order to turn a photograph into a form suitable for FOUR COLOR PRINTING, it has to be separated into four image components: cyan, magenta, yellow and black. Today, this is normally done by an electro-optical device called a scanner. Increasingly, black and white HALF TONES are also scanned for reproduction, instead of using the old SCREENING process.

Scatter Proofs

When pictures are prepared for reproduction, the first proofs are normally "scattered" on a large sheet of paper. Only when the pictures have been approved are they cut up and placed on the pages in the positions that they will occupy in the final book. In this form, they are called IMPOSED PROOFS.

Screening

HALF-TONES are prepared for printing by "screening," which reduces shades of gray to a form in which they can be printed. See Section 8.1.4.

Separations

See SCANNING.

Set Off Disk

If the author wrote the original manuscript using a word processor, it may be possible to "milk" the disk containing the text and to set the type from the electronic information on the disk. This is known as "setting off disk," and is very useful because it saves time and money, and removes the likelihood of errors being introduced by the typesetter.

Setting

See TYPESETTING.

"Slush Pile"   The "slush pile" is the stack of unsolicited manuscripts that are sent to almost all publishers and agents. It is at least nine-tenths rubbish, and often nine hundred and ninety nine thousandths rubbish, but there is always the hope that somewhere in there, a brilliant manuscript is waiting to be discovered.

Spot Color   "Spot color" is color without tone: solid color. In order to introduce (say) a pink instead of a red, you would have to change the ink color. If you use a TONE SCREEN, though, you can introduce tones of a particular color.

Subject Matter Expert For a non-fiction book, it is not unusual to ask an acknowledged expert in the field to read the MANUSCRIPT to make sure that it is accurate — but he or she is not normally expected to make judgements of literary merit.

Tone Screens   Imagine a solid red. Now, break it down into dots. The more dots, the more solid the tone. An "eighty per cent tone" is a much deeper red than a "twenty per cent tone," which is more like a pale pink.

Trade Names   Many words in common use, like "Xerox" or "Hoover" or "Frigidaire" or "Kleenex" are registered trade names, and must appear with a capital letter. The COPYEDITOR should check that this is done, or else substitute "generic" terms such as "photo-copy" or "vacuum cleaner" or "refrigerator" or "paper tissue."

Typescript   Strictly, if a MANUSCRIPT is not hand-written, it is not a manuscript; but type-written material (strictly a "typescript") is commonly referred to as a manuscript too.

Typesetting   The typesetter takes the MARKED-UP TYPESCRIPT after the COPYEDITOR and EDITOR have finished with it, and KEYS IT IN to a typesetting machine. The printout from the typesetting machine (which may be a HOT-METAL LINOTYPE or a PHOTOTYPESETTER) is used to create the type as it will appear in the final book.

Underlining   Text that is underlined in a TYPESCRIPT should be in italics when it is typeset.

APPENDICES

APPENDIX 1

PARTIAL LISTING OF CHILDREN'S AND YOUNG ADULT

BOOK PUBLISHERS

The following list is comprised of publishers who either specialize in children's and/or young adult books, or who have a division which publishes books for younger people. Some of these publishers may use the services of freelance proofreaders, editors, etc. *REMEMBER* when you submit a letter of inquiry to *make sure that you let them know you don't expect a reply from them* unless they have work available.

Academic Therapy Publications
20 Commercial Boulevard
Novato, CA 94949

Addison Wesley Publishing Co.
Route 128
Reading, MA 01867

Alaska Northwest Books
22026 20 Ave SE
Bothell, WA 98021

Anchorage Press Inc.
Box 8067
New Orleans, LA 70182

Anthroposophic Press Inc.
Box 94-A-1, RR 4
Hudson, NY 12534

Antioch Publishing Co.
888 Dayton Street
Yellow Springs, OH 45387

Appalachian Consortium Press
University Hall
Appalachian State University
Boone, NC 28608

Appalachian Mountain Club
Books
5 Joy Street
Boston, MA 02108

Arte Publico Press
University of Houston
M.D. Anderson Library, Room 2
Houston, TX 77204

Associated Features, Inc.
Box 1762 Murray Hill Station
New York, NY 10156

**Association For Research &
Enlightenment, Inc.**
Box 595, 67 Street & Atlantic Ave.
Virginia Beach, VA 23451

Atheneum Publishers
866 Third Avenue
New York, NY 10022

Atrium Publications
Box 938
Ojai, CA 93024

Authors Connection Press
710 NW 23rd Avenue
Gainesville, FL 32609

Avon Books
105 Madison Avenue
New York, NY 10016

Backpax International Ltd.
Box 603
Wilton, CT 06897

Ball-stick-bird Publications
Box 592
Stony Brook, NY 11790

Bantam Books
666 Fifth Avenue
New York, NY 10103

Barron's Education Series, Inc.
250 Wireless Blvd.
Hauppauge, NY 11788

BDD Promotional Book Co, Inc.
666 Fifth Avenue
New York, NY 10103

Beautiful America Publishing Co.
9725 SW Commerce Circle
Wilsonville, OR 97070

Peter Bedrick Books, Inc.
2112 Broadway, Suite 318
New York, NY 10023

Bellerophon Books
36 Anacapa Street
Santa Barbara, CA 93101

Beyond Words Publishing, Inc.
Box 492 B Route 3
Hillsboro, OR 97123

Bradbury Press
866 Third Avenue
New York, NY 10022

Camelot Publishing Co.
Box 1357
Ormond Beach, FL 32175

Camex Books, Inc.
535 Firth Avenue
New York, NY 10017

Career Publishing Inc.
Box 5486
Orange, CA 92613

Carolrhoda Books, Inc.
241 First Avenue North
Minneapolis, MN 55401

Charlesbridge Publishing
85 Main Street
Watertown, MA 02172

Children's Book Press
1339 61st Street
Emeryville, CA 94608

Childrens Press
5440 N. Cumberland Ave.
Chicago, IL 60656

Child's Play
137 E. 25th St. 9th Floor
New York, NY 10010

Chronicle Books
275 Fifth Avenue
San Francisco, CA 94103

Clarion Books
215 Park Avenue South
New York, NY 10003

Cliff Notes, Inc.
Box 80728
Lincoln, NE 68501

David C. Cook Publishing
850 N. Grove Ave.
Elgin, IL 60120

Crabtree Publishing Co.
350 Fifth Ave., Ste. 3308
New York, NY 10118

Creative Education Inc.
Box 227, 123 S. Broad St.
Mankato, MN 56001

Dell Publishing
666 Fifth Ave.
New York, NY 10103

Dillon Press, Inc.
242 Portland Ave. S.
Minneapolis, MN 55415

Discovery Enterprises, Ltd.
134 Middle St., Ste. 210
Lowell, MA 01852

DLM
One DLM Park
Allen, TX 75002

EP Dutton
375 Hudson St
New York, Ny 10014

Enslow Publishers
Box 777, Bloy St. & Ramsey Ave.
Hillside, NJ 07205

M. Evans & Co., Inc.
216 E. 49th Street
New York, NY 10017

Gannett Books
390 Congress St.
Portland, ME 04104

Gareth Stevens, Inc.
Rivercenter Bldg., Ste. 201
1555 N. Rivercenter Dr.
Milwaukee, WI 53212

Garrett Educational Corp.
Box 1588, 130 E. 13 S.
Ada, OK 74820

The C R Gibson Co.
32 Knight St.
Norwalk, CT 06856

David R. Godine, Publisher Inc.
Horticultural Hall
300 Massachusetts Ave.
Boston, MA 02115

Green Tiger Press
435 E. Carmel Street
San Marcos, CA 92069

Greenwillow Books
105 Madison Ave.
New York, NY 10016

Harper Collins Publishers
10 E. 53 St.
New York, NY 10022

Harrison House Publishers
1029 N. Utica
Tulsa, OK 74110

Hazelden Publishing Group
Box 176
Center City, MN 55012

Heartstone Press Inc.
Box 890686
Houston, TX 77289

Heian International Inc.
Box 1013
Union City, CA 94587

Jim Henson Productions
117E 69 Street
New York, NY 10021

Holiday House Inc.
40 E. 49th Street
New York, NY 10017

Henry Holt & Co., Inc.
115 W. 18th Street
New York, NY 10011

Houghton Mifflin Co.
One Beacon St.
Boston, MA 02108

Ideals Publishing Corp
Box 140300
565 Marriott Dr. Ste. 890
Nashville, TN 37214

Impact Publishers
Box 1094
San Luis Obispo, CA 93406

Kaleidoscopix Inc.
Box 389
Franklin, MA 02038

Kane/Miller Book Publishers
Box 529
Brooklyn, NY 11231

Kidsbooks, Inc.
7004 N. California Ave.
Chicago, IL 60645

Kitchen Sink Press, Inc.
2 Swamp Rd.
Princeton, WI 54968

Alfred A. Knopf Inc.
201 E. 50 Street
New York, NY 10022

Ladybird Books, Inc.
Box 1690 49 Omni Circle
Auburn, ME 04210

Learning Links, Inc.
2300 Marcus Ave.
New Hyde Park, NY 11042

Lerner Publications
241 First Ave. N.
Minneapolis, MN 55401

Lion Publishing Corp.
1705 Hubbard Ave.
Batavia, IL 60510

Little, Brown, & Co., Inc.
34 Beacon St.
Boston, MA 02108

The Millbrook Press
2 Old New Milford Rd.
Brookfield, CT 06804

Milliken Publishing Co.
1100 Research Blvd.
St. Louis, MO 63132

Modern Publishing
155 E. 55 Street
New York, NY 10022

Joshua Morris Publishing Co.
221 Danbury Rd.
Wilton, CT 06897

Morrow Junior Books
105 Madison Avenue
New York, NY 10016

Multnomah Press
10209 S.E. Division St.
Portland, OR 97266

Oddo Publishing Inc.
Box 68 Storybook Acres
Fayetteville, GA 30214

Orchard Books
387 Park Ave. S.
New York, NY 10016

Ottenheimer Publishers, Inc.
300 Reistertown Rd.
Baltimore, MD 21208

Paraclete Press
Box 1568
Orleans, MA 02653

Parents Magazine Press
685 Third Ave.
New York, NY 10017

Pippin Press
Box 92 Gracie Station
229 E. 85th Street
New York, NY 10028

Playmore Inc., Publishers
1107 Broadway
New York, NY 10010

Price Stern Sloan, Inc.
360 N. La Cienega Blvd.
Los Angeles, CA 90048

The Putnam Berkley Group, Inc.
200 Madison Ave.
New York, NY 10016

Raintree Publishers
310 Wisconsin Ave.
Milwaukee, WI 53203

Running Press Book Publishers
125 S. 22 Street
Philadelphia, PA 19103

Scholastic Inc.
730 Broadway
New York, NY 10003

Sentinel Books
633 N. Orange Ave.
Orlando, FL 32801

Shengold Publishers, Inc.
18 W. 45 Street
New York, NY 10036

The Shoe String Press, Inc.
Box 4327
Hamden, CT 06514

Sierra Club Books
100 Bush Street
San Francisco, CA 94104

Silver Burdett Press Inc.
190 Sylvan Avenue
Englewood Cliffs, NJ 07632

Stoneway Ltd.
Box 548
Southeastern, PA 19399

Troll Associates
100 Corporate Dr.
Mahwah, NJ 07430

Tuffy Books
200 Madison Ave.
New York, NY 10016

Twenty First Century Books
38 S. Market Street
Frederick, MD 21701

The Unicorn Publishing House, Inc.
120 American Rd.
Morris Plains, NJ 07950

Walker & Co.
720 Fifth Avenue
New York, NY 10019

Warner Books, Inc.
666 Fifth Avenue
New York, NY 10103

Waterfront Books
98 Brookes Avenue
Burlington, VT 05401

Franklin Watts, Inc.
387 Park Avenue South
New York, NY 10016

Daniel Weiss Associates, Inc.
33 W. 17th Street
New York, NY 10011

Western Publishing Co, Inc.
Golden Books For Children
850 Third Avenue
New York, NY 10022

Albert Whitman & Co.
5747 W. Howard St.
Niles, IL 60648

World Book Inc.
525 W. Monroe, 20th Floor
Chicago, IL 60606

Young Discovery Library
217 Main Street
Ossining, NY 10562

APPENDIX 2

PARTIAL LISTING OF PUBLISHERS

OF BOOKS ON TAPE

The following companies use the AUDIO CASSETTE format for some (or all) of their publications. If you are interested in finding out whether they use the services of freelance people, your best bet would be to send them a query letter, asking whether or not they utilize freelancers to voice any of their tapes. If you get a positive response, then you can submit a demo tape of your work. We have found in dealing with most publishing companies, it is best if you *mention somewhere in the content of your correspondence that they need reply ONLY if they use the services in question.* The men and women working in this industry are extremely busy, so it is a courtesy on your part if you let them know you don't expect a reply unless they could potentially use your services. Books being read onto audio cassettes is still a very young offshoot of the publishing trade. Although many of these companies may be small, or currently have very few audio publications, within the next few years this could change dramatically.

AASLH Press
172 N. Second Ave., Ste. 202
Nashville, TN 37201

Abbey Press
Hill Dr.
Meinrad, IN 47577

Ability Workshop Press
Attn: Melinda Dewey
24861 Alicia Pkwy., No. 292
Laguna Hills, CA 92653

American Bar Association
750 N. Lake Shore Dr.
Chicago, IL 60611

American Institute of C.P.A.'s
1211 Ave. of the Americas
New York, NY 10036

Amity House
16 High Street
Warwick, NJ 10990

Ariel Press
3854 Mason Rd.
Canal Winchester, OH 43110

Association for Research & Enlightenment, Inc.
Box 595
Virginia Beach, VA 23451

Astronomical Society of the Pacific
390 Ashton Avenue
San Francisco, CA 94112

Ave Maria Press
Notre Dame, IN 46556

Backpax International, Ltd.
Box 603
Wilton, CT 06897

Balcony Publishing
3011 N. Hwy 620
Austin, TX 78734

Baptist Spanish Publishing House
7000 Alabama
El Paso, TX 79914

Barron's Educational Services
250 Wireless Blvd.
Hauppauge, NY 11788

The Benjamin Co., Inc.
One Westchester Plaza
Elmsford, NY 10523

Bolchazy-Carducci Publishers
1000 Brown St., Unit 101
Wauconda, IL 60084

Brandon House Inc.
Box 240
Bronx, NY 10471

Cinco Puntos Press
2709 Louisville
El Paso, TX 79930

Communication Creativity
Box 909
Buena Vista, CO 81211

Copyright Information Services
Box 1460-A
Friday Harbor, WA 98250

Cornerstone Large Print Books
Box 1911, 130 Cremona Dr.
Santa Barbara, CA 93116

Council of State Governments
Box 11910
Iron Works Pike
Lexington, KY 40578

Cross Cultural Publications
Box 506
Notre Dame, IN 46556

Cynthia Publishing Co.
BOX 2030
Los Angeles, CA 90046

Don Bosco Multimedia
Box T, 475 North Avenue
New Rochelle, NY 10802

EDL
Box 210726
Columbia, SC 29221

Educational Insights, Inc.
19560 S. Rancho Way
Dominguez Hills, CA 90220

Festival Publications
BOX 4940
West Hills, CA 91304

Georgetown University Press
Intercultural Center, Room 111
Washington, DC 20057

Gessler Publishing Co., Inc.
55 W. 13th St.
New York, NY 10011

G.K. Hall & Co.
70 Lincoln Street
Boston, MA 02111

Hay House, Inc.
501 Santa Monica Blvd., Ste. 602
Santa Monica, CA 90404

Her Own Words
Box 5264 Hilldale
Madison, WI 53705

**Herodinius Enlightened Life
Publications**
Box 2925
Orange, CA 92669

Human Energy Press
370 W. San Bruno Ave., Suite D
San Bruno, CA 94066

Humanics LTD
1389 N.E. Peachtree St., Ste. 370
Atlanta, GA 30309

Huntington House, Inc.
Box 53788
Lafayette, LA 70505

Ignatius Press
2515 McAllister Street
San Francisco, CA 94118

Inner Vision Publishing
Box 1117
Seapines Station
Virginia Beach, VA 23451

**Jewish Braille Institute of
America, Inc.**
110 E. 30 Street
New York, NY 10016

Bob Jones University Press
1700 Wade Hampton Blvd.
Greenville, SC 29614

Klutz Press
2121 Staunton Court
Palo Alto, CA 94306

Life Action Press
902 S. Burnside Ave.
Los Angeles, CA 90036

Life Survival Digest Inc.
Box 3256
Austin, TX 78764

**Life Rhythm/Multi-Media
Products**
Box 806
Mendocino, CA 95460

Liguori Publications
One Liguori Drive
Liguori, MO 63057

Linch Publishing, Inc.
Box 75
Orlando, FL 32802

Linton Day Publishing
4816 Kenilworth Dr.
Stone Mountain, GA 30083

Llewellyn Publications
Box 64383
St. Paul, MN 55164

Longman, Inc.
Longman Bldg, 95 Church St.
White Plains, NY 10601

Longstreet Press
2150 Newmarket Pkwy, Suite 102
Marietta, GA 30067

Lotus Light Publication
Box 2
Wilmot, WI 53192

McGraw-Hill, Inc.
1221 Ave. of the Americas
New York, NY 10020

Mage Publishers, Inc.
1032 N.W. 29 Street
Washington, DC 20007

Mastermedia, Ltd.
215 Park Ave. S., Ste. 1601
New York, NY 10003

Metamorphous Press
3249 N.W. 29 Ave.
Portland, OR 97210

Minnesota
690 Cedar St.
St. Paul, MN 55101

Morehouse Publishing Co.
78 Danbury Rd.
Wilton, CT 06897

Multi Media Arts
BOX 14486
Austin, TX 78761

Multnomah Press
10209 S.E. Division St.
Portland, OR 97266

New Creation Publishing Group
Box 763
Stone Ridge, NY 12484

New Dimensions in Education
50 Executive Blvd.
Elmsford, NY 10523

Northword Press, Inc.
Box 1360
Minocqua, WI 54548

Oceana Publications, Inc.
75 Main Street
Dobbs Ferry, NY 10522

Outlet Book Co.
225 S. Park Avenue
New York, NY 10003

Palace Publishing
Road 1, Box 320
Moundsville, WV 26041

Paradon Publishing Co.
Box 10209
Minneapolis, MN 55458

Parallax Press
Box 7355
Berkeley, CA 94707

Parkside Publishing
205 W. Touhy Avenue
Park Ridge, IL 60068

Pasport Books
4255 W. Touhy Avenue
Lincolnwood, IL 60646

Penguin U.S.A.
375 Hudson Street
New York, NY 10014

Practice Management Assoc.
10 Midland Avenue
Newton, MA 02158

Practicing Management Assoc.
810 Seventh Avenue
New York, NY 10019

Productivity Press
BOX 3007
Cambridge, MA 02140

Professional Publications
1250 Fifth Avenue
Belmont, CA 94002

Research Press
2612 N. Mattis Avenue
Champaign, IL 61821

Rudra Press
Box 1973
Cambridge, MA 02238

Scripture Press Publications
1825 College Avenue
Wheaton, IL 60187

Seal Press
3131 Western Ave., Ste. 410
Seattle, WA 98121

Seal Press
300 Massachusetts Ave.
Boston, MA 02115

Simon & Schuster
1230 Ave. of the Americas
New York, NY 10020

Soundprints Corporation
165 Water Street
Norwalk, CT 06856

Spectran Publishing
Box 467637
Atlanta, GA 30346

Spoken Arts, Inc.
310 North Street
New Rochelle, NY 10801

Storey/Garden Way Publishing
Schoolhouse Road
Pownal, VT 05261

Theosophical Publishing House
306 W. Geneva Road
Wheaton, IL 60187

Timeless Books
Box 50905
Palo Alto, CA 94303

The Vestal Press, Ltd.
Box 97
Vestal, NY 13851

Wayside Publishing
129 Commonwealth Ave.
Concord, MA 01742

Wilshire Book Co.
12015 Sherman Road
North Hollywood, CA 91605

Wingbow Press
2929 Fifth Street
Berkeley, CA 94710

Word, Inc.
5221 N. O'Connor Blvd., Ste. 1000
Irving, TX 75039

Youth Education Systems
Box 223
Scarborough Station
BriarCliff Manor, NY 10510

Zondervan Publishing
1415 S.E. Lake Dr.
Grand Rapids, MI 49506

APPENDIX 3

SOME CANADIAN PUBLISHING HOUSES

The following is a partial listing of Canadian publishers. Although they may be in need of your services, when you write to them *IT IS VERY IMPORTANT* for you to acknowledge in your letter that you **do not expect to hear from them** unless they do, indeed, have work for you. Remember, you are "selling" your services to them, and a very important part of selling is respect for another's valuable time and priorities.

Acta Press
Subs of Icord Ltd.
Box 3243, Postal Sta B
Calgary, AB T2M 4L8
Canada
Publish in English, with some French & German.

Addison-Wesley Publishers Ltd.
Box 580, 26 Prince Andrew Place
Don Mills, ON M3C 2T8
Canada
Publish in English & French.

Agence D'Arc Inc. Editions
Subs of Les Editions HRW Ltee
8023 rue Jarry Est
Montreal, PQ H1J 1H6
Canada
Publish in French.

Annick Press Ltd.
15 Patricia Avenue
Willowdale, ON M2M1H9
Canada
Children's books. Publish in English & French.

Ballantine Books of Canada
Div of Random House of Canada Ltd.
1265 Aerowood Drive
Mississauga, ON L4W 1B9
Canada
Publish in English.

Black Rose Books Ltd.
3981 St Laurent Blvd, 4th fl, Suite 444
Montreal, PQ H2W 1Y5
Canada
Publish in English.

The Boston Mills Press
Div of One Man's Way Ltd.
132 Main Street
Erin, ON N0B 1T0
Canada
Publish in English

Breakwater Books Ltd.
Box 2188, 100 Water Street
St Johns, NF A1C 6E6
Canada
Publish in English.

Brimar Publishing/Tormont Publication Inc.
338 St Antoine E
Montreal, PQ H2Y 1A3
Canada
Publish in English & French

Butterworths Canada Ltd.
Subs of Butterworth & Co. Ltd.
Div of Reed International PLC
75 Clegg Road
Markham, ON L6G 1A1
Canada
Publish in English & French.

Canada Law Book Inc.
Subs of Canada Law Book Holdings Ltd.
240 Edwards Street
Aurora, ON L4G 3S9
Canada
Publish in English.

Canada Publishing Corp.
164 Commander Blvd
Agincourt, ON M1S 3C7
Canada
Publish in English.

Canadian Museum of Civilization
Box 3100, 100 Laurier Street, Sta B
Hull, PQ J8X 4H2
Canada
Publish in English & French

CCH Canadian Ltd.
Subs of Commerce Clearing House Inc
6 Garamond Court
Don Mills, ON M3C 1Z5
Canada
Publish in English & French

Centax Books & Distribution
Div of M C Graphics Inc.
1048 Fleury Street
Regina, SK S4N 4W8
Canada
Publish in English

Le Cercle du Livre de France Ltee
Editions Pierre Tisseyr
8925 boul St Laurent
Montreal, PQ H2N 1M5
Canada
Publish in French.
****

Coach House Press
401 Huron Street (rear)
Toronto, ON M5S 2G5
Canada
Publish in English.

Collier Macmillan Canada Inc.
Subs of Macmillan Publishing Co. Inc.
1200 Eglinton Avenue E
Don Mills, ON M3C 3N1
Canada
Publish in English.

Copp Clark Pitman Ltd.
Subs of Longman Group
2775 Matheson Blvd E
Mississauga, ON L4W 4P7
Canada
Publish in English.

La Courte Echelle
5243 St Laurence Blvd
Montreal, PQ H2T 1S4
Canada
Publish in English & French.

Louise Courteau, Editrice Inc.
7433 rue St-Denis
Montreal, PQ H2R 2E5
Canada
Publish in French.

Crabtree Publishing Co. Ltd.
1110 Kamato Road, Unit 4
Mississauga, ON L4W 2P3
Canada
Publish in English.

Creative Publishers
Div of Robinson-Blackmore Printing
& Publishing Ltd.
36 Austin Street
St Johns, NF A1B 3T7
Canada
Publish in English.

Detselig Enterprises Ltd.
Box G399
Calgary, AB T3A 2G3
Canada
Publish in English

Diffullvre Inc.
817 rue McCaffrey
Saint-Laurent, PQ H4T 1N3
Canada
Publish in French.

Doubleday Canada Ltd.
105 Bond Street
Toronto, ON M5B 1Y3
Canada
Publish in English.

Douglas & McIntyre Ltd.
1615 Venables Street
Vancouver, BC V5L 2H1
Canada
Publish in English.

Dundurn Press Ltd.
2181 Queen Street E, Suite 301
Toronto, ON MYE 1E5
Canada
Publish in English.

Durkin Hayes Publishing Ltd.
3312 Mainway
Burlington, ON L7M 1A7
Canada
Publish in English & French.

Ecrits des Forges
903 St Thomas
Trois Rivieres, PQ G9A 5G4
Canada
Publish in French.

ECW Press
307 Coxwell Avenue
Toronto, ON M4L 3B5
Canada
Publish in English.

Edilvre Inc. Diffusion Soussan
5518 Ferrier
Ville Mont-Royal, PQ H4P 1M2
Canada
Publish in English & French.

Editions Beauchemin Ltee
3281 Avenue Jean Beraud
Chomedey Laval, PQ H7T 2L2
Canada
Publish in French.

**Editions Broquet Inc./Broquet
Publishing Co. Inc.**
CP 310
La Prairie, PQ J5R 3Y3
Canada
Publish in French & English.

Les editions Chouette
CP 519 succursale C
Montreal, PQ H2L 4K4
Canada
Publish in English & French.

Les Editions D'Acadle
CP 885, 27 rue John
Moncton, NB E1C 8N8
Canada
Publish in French.

Les Editions de la Pleine Lune
CP 188, Succursale de Lorimier
Montreal, PQ H2H 2N6
Canada
Publish in French.

Editions de l'Hexagone
900 rue Ontario est
Montreal, PQ H2L 1P4
Canada
Publish in French.

Les Editions de l'Homme
Div of Sogides
955 rue Amherst
Montreal, PQ H2L 3K4
Canada
Publish in French.

Les Editions du Boreal
4447 Sr Denis
Montreal, PQ H2J 2L2
Canada
Publish in French.

**Editions du Renouveau Pedagoglque
Inc.**
8925 boul St Laurent
Montreal, PQ H2N 1M5
Canada
Publish in French.

Editions du Septentrion
1300 av Maguire
Sillery, PQ G1T 1Z3
Canada
Publish in French & some English.

Editions du Trocarre
817, rue McCaffrey
Saint-Laurent, PQ H4T 1N3
Canada
Publish in French.

Editions Fides
165 rue Deslauriers
St Laurent, PQ H4N 2S4
Canada
Publish in French.

Editions FM
Div of Creabec International Inc.
1113 Desnoyers Avenue, St Vincent-
de-Paul
Ville de Laval, PQ H7C 1Y6
Canada
Publish in French.

Editions Hurtubise HMH Ltee
7360 boul Newman
Ville La Salle, PQ H8N 1X2
Canada
Publish in French.

**Les Editions Internationales Alsin
Stanke Ltd.**
1212 Mathieu Street
Montreal PQ H3H 2H7
Canada
Publish in French.

Editions Parti Pris
Subs of Editions de l'Hexagone
900 est, rue Ontario
Montreal, PQ H2L 1P4
Canada
Publish in French.

Les Editions Yvon Blais Inc.
Div of Butterworths Canada
BP 180
Cowansville, PQ J2K 3H6
Canada
Publish in English & French.

H B Fenn & Co. Ltd.
2455 Lucknow Drive
Mississauga, ON L5S 1H9
Canada
Publish in English.

Fifth House Publishers
20 36 Street E
Saskatoon, SK S7K 5S8
Canada
Publish in English.

Fraser Institute
626 Bute Street
Vancouver, BC V6E 3M1
Canada
Publish in English.

Gaetan Morin Editeur Ltee
175 Bld de Mortagne
Boucherville, PQ J4B 6G4
Canada
Publish in English & French.

General Paperbacks
Div of General Publishing Co. Ltd.
34 Lesmill Road
Don Mills, ON M3B 2T6
Canada
Publish in English.

General Publishing Co. Ltd.
30 Lesmill Road
Don Mills, ON M3B 2T6
Canada
Publish in English.

Globe/Modern Curriculum Press
Div of Prentice-Hall Canada
3771 Victoria Park Avenue
Scarborough, ON M1W 2P9
Canada
Publish in English & French.

Grolier Ltd. - Grolier Ltee
Subs of Grolier Inc.
16 Overlea Blvd
Toronto, ON M4H 1A6
Canada
Publish in English & French.

Groundwood Gooks Ltd.
Div of Douglas & McIntyre
585 Bloor Street W
Toronto, ON M6G 1K5
Canada
Publish in English.

Guerin Editeur Ltee
4501 rue Drolet
Montreal, PQ H2T 2G2
Canada
Publish in French & some English.

Hancock House Publishers Ltd.
19313 Zero Avenue
Surrey, BC V3S 5J9
Canada
Publish in English.

Harlequin Enterprises Ltd.
Subs of Torstar Corp.
225 Duncan Mill Road
Don Mills, ON M3B 3K9
Canada
Publish in English & French.

Harper Collins Publishers Ltd.
55 Avenue Road, Suite 2900, Hazelton
Toronto, ON M5R 3L2
Canada
Publish in English.

The Frederick Harris Music Co. Ltd.
529 Speers Road
Oakville, On L6K 2G4
Canada
Publish in English & French.

D C Heath Canada Ltd.
100 Adelaide Street W, Suite 1600
Toronto, On M5H 1S9
Canada
French; school textbook.

Herald Press
Div of Mennonite Publishing House
Inc.
490 Dutton Drive
Waterloo, ON N2L 6H7
Canada
Publish in English.

C J Hogrefe & Huber Inc.
Subs of Verlag fuer Psychologie (Fed
Rep of Germany)
12 Bruce Park Avenue
Toronto, ON M4P 2S3
Canada
Publish in English.

**Holt, Rinehart & Winston of Canada
Ltd.**
55 Horner Avenue
Toronto, ON M8Z 4X6
Canada
Publish in English.

Hans Huber Publishers Inc.
Subs of Verlag Hans Huber
(Swizerland)
14 Bruce Park Avenue
Toronto, ON M4P 2S3
Canada
Publish in English.

**The Institute for Research on Public
Policy**
275 Slater Street, 5th fl
Ottawa, ON K1P 5H9
Canada
Publish in English & French.

**International Development Research
Center**
Box 8500, 250 Albert Street
Ottawa, ON K1G 3H9
Canada
Publish in English & French.

Irwin Publishing
Div of Stoddart/General Publishing
Co. Ltd.
1800 Steels Avenue W
Concord, ON L4K 2P3
Canada
Publish in English & some French.

Kamin & Howell Inc.
48 Michael Court
Thornhill, ON L4J 3A9
Canada
Publish in English & French.

Kids Can Press Ltd.
585½ Bloor Street W
Toronto, ON M6G 1K5
Canada
Publish in English.

Lancelot Press Ltd.
Box 425
Hantsport, NS B0P 1P0
Canada
Publish in English.

Lemeac Editeur
3575 boul Saint Laurent, Suite 902
Montreal, PQ H2X 2T7
Canada
Publish in French.

Lester & Orpen Dennys Ltd.
78 Sullivan Street
Toronto, ON M5T 1C1
Canada
Publish in English.

Lidec Inc.
4350 Avenue de l'Hotel-de-Ville
Montreal, PQ H2W 2H5
Canada
Publish in French.

James Lorimer & Co. Ltd., Publishers
Egerton Ryerson Memorial Bldg
35 Britain Street
Toronto, ON M5A 1R7
Canada
Publish in English.

McClelland & Stewart Inc.
481 University Avenue, Suite 900
Toronto, ON M5G 2E9
Canada
Publish in English.

McClelland-Bantam Inc.
105 Bond Street
Toronto, ON M5B 1Y3
Canada
Publish in English.

McGill-Queen's University Press
3430 McTavish Street
Montreal, PQ 83A 1X9
Canada
Publish in English & French.

McGraw Hill, Editeurs
750 boul Laurentien
Ville St-Laurent, PQ H4M 2M4
Canada
Publish in French.

McGraw-Hill Ryerson Ltd.
Subs of McGraw-Hill Inc.
300 Water Street
Whitby, ON LIN 9B6
Canada
Publish in English & French.

Macmillan of Canada
Div of Canada Publishing Corp.
29 Birch Avenue, Toronto, ON M4V
1E2
Canada
Publish in English.

Michelin Maps & Guides
Subs of Michelin Tires Canada Ltd.
175 boul Bouchard
Dorval, PQ H9S 5T1
Canada
Publish in English & French.

Micromedia Ltd.
158 Pearl Street
Toronto, ON M5H 1L3
Canada
Publish in English & French.

Modulo Editeur Inc.
233 Avenue Dunbar, Rm 300
Mont Royal, PQ H3P 2H4
Canada
Publish in English & French.

Mosaic Press
Box 1032
Oakville, ON L6J 5E9
Canada
Publish in English.

Mosby-Year Book Limited
Subs of Mosby-Year Book Inc.
5240 Finch Avenue E
Scarborough, ON M1S 5A2
Canada
Publish in English.

Musson Publishing
Div of General Publishing Co. Ltd.
30 Lesmill Road
Don Mills, ON M2B 2T6
Canada
Publish in English.

Nelson Canada
Div of Thomson Canada Ltd.
1120 Birchmount Road
Scarborough, ON M1K 5G4
Canada
Publish in English.

Nimbus Publishing Ltd.
Subs of H H Marshall Ltd.
Box 9301, Sta A
Halifax, NS B3K 5N5
Canada
Publish in English.

North-South Institute/Institut Nord-Sud
55 Murray, Suite 200
Ottawa, ON K1N 5M3
Canada
Publish in English & French.

Novalis
Div of Unimedia
6255 Hutchinson
Montreal, PQ H2V 4S7
Canada
Publish in English & French.

Oberon Press
Div of Michael Hardy Ltd.
350 Sparks Street, Ste 400
Ottawa, ON K1R 7S8
Canada
Publish in English.

OISE Press/Guidance Centre
Div of The Ontario Institute for
Studies in Education
252 Bloor Street W
Toronto, ON M5S 1V6
Canada
Publish in English & French.

Orca Book Publishers Ltd.
Box 5626, Sta B
Victoria, BC V8R 6S4
Canada
Publish in English.

Oxford University Press Canada
Subs of Oxford University Press
70 Wynford Drive
Don Mills, ON M3C 1J9
Canada
Publish in English & French.

Peace Research Institute-Dundas
25 Dundana Avenue
Dundas, ON L9H 4E5
Canada
Publish in English.

Peguls Publishers Ltd.
520 Hargrave Street
Winnipeg, MB R3A 0X8
Canada
Publish in English.

Penguin Books Canada Ltd.
Subs of The Penguin Publishing Co.
Ltd.
2801 John Street
Markham, ON L3R 1B4
Canada
Publish in English.

Pippin Publishing Ltd.
1361 Huntingwood Drive, Unit 7
Agincourt, ON M1S 3J1
Canada
Publish in English & French.

Prentice-Hall Canada Inc.
Subs of Simon & Schuster
Div. of Paramount Comm. Inc.
1870 Birchmount Road
Scarborough, ON M1P 2J7
Canada
Publish in English.

Les Presses de L'Universite de Montreal
CP 6128, Sue A
Montreal, PQ H3C 3J7
Canada
Publish in French.

Les Presses de l'Universite du Quebec
2875 boul Laurier
Ste-Foy, PQ G1V 2M3
Canada
Publish in English & French

Les Publications Graflcor 1989 Inc.
Subs of Groupe Morin
175 boul de Mortagne
Boucherville, PQ J4B 6G4
Canada
Publish in French.

Reader's Digest Association (Canada) Ltd./Selection du Reader's Digest (Canada) Ltee
215 Redfern Avenue
Westmount, PQ H3Z 2V9
Canada
Publish in English & French.

Reid Publishing Ltd.
Box 7267
Oakville, ON L6J 6L6
Canada
Publish in English.

Scholastic Canada Ltd.
Subs of Scholastic Inc. (USA)
123 Newkirk Road
Richmond Hill, ON L4C 3G5
Canada
Publish in English & French.

Seal Books
105 Bond STREET
Toronto, ON M5B 1Y3
Canada
Publish in English.

Sogides Ltee
955 rue Amherst
Montreal, PQ H2L 3K4
Canada
Publish in French.

Stoddart Publishing Co. Ltd.
Subs of General Publishing Co. Ltd.
34 Lesmill Road
Don Mills, ON M3B 2T6
Canada
Publish in English.

Summerhill Press Ltd.
52 Shaftesbury Avenue
Toronto, ON M4T 1A2
Canada
Publish in English.

Trinity Press
Div of Triwel Publishing House
The Gateway
Burlington, ON L7L 5K7
Canada
Publish in English.

University of British Columbia Press
303-6344 Memorial Road
Vancouver, BC V6T 1W5
Canada
Publish in English.

University of Ottawa Press/Les Presses de l'Universite d'Ottawa
603 Cumberland
Ottawa, ON K1N 6N5
Canada
Publish in English & French.

University of Toronto Press
10 St Mary Street, Suite 700
Toronto, ON M4Y 2W8
Canada
Publish in English.

VLB Editeur Inc.
1339 Avenue Lajole
Outremont, PQ H2V 1P6
Canada
Publish in French.

G R Welch Co. Ltd.
Div of Triwel Publishing House
The Gateway
Burlington, ON L7L 5K7
Canada
Publish in English.

Whitecap Books Ltd.
1086 W Third Street
North Vancouver, BC V7P 3J6
Canada
Publish in English & some French.

Whitman Golden Ltd.
Subs of Western Publishing Inc.
200 Sheldon Drive
Cambridge, ON N1R 5X2
Canada
Publish in English.

John Wiley & Sons Canada Ltd.
Subs of John Wiley & Sons Inc. (USA)
22 Worcester Road
Rexdale, ON M9W 1L1
Canada
Publish in English & French.

Wilfrid Laurier University Press
Alumni Hall, Wilifrid Laurier
University
Waterloo, ON N2L 3C5
Canada
Publish in English & French.

Worldwide Library
Div of Harlequin Enterprises Ltd.
225 Duncan Mill Road
Don Mills, ON M3B 3K9
Canada
Publish in English.

APPENDIX 4

EMPLOYMENT AGENCIES

The following is a list of employment agencies specializing in the publishing trade. Please note that we have no affiliation with any of these companies, and strongly urge you to check with the Better Business Bureau prior to using their services.

Able Personnel Agency, Inc.
280 Madison Avenue
New York, NY 10016

Places editors, writers, proofreaders, editorial assistants, personnel staff, etc.

Helen Akullian Agency Inc.
280 Madison Ave., Room 604
New York, NY 10016

Specializes in placement for all levels in editorial, marketing, promotion/copywriting, etc.

Associated Writing Programs
Old Dominion University
Norfolk, VA 23529

Publish job lists & provide job placement for writers.

Breffington Inc.
134 W. 71 Street
New York, NY 10023

Specialize in placing editorial, production, art, marketing, advertising, promotion, administrative & financial staff.

Communicators Connection Inc.
7638 Holmes Run Dr.
Falls Church, VA 22042

Recruit permanent & temporary publications specialists for the metropolitan Washington, DC area.

Bert Davis Associates, Inc.
400 Madison Avenue
New York, NY 10017

Recruit nationwide for personnel from entry level to CEO in editorial, book sales, ad space sales, production, etc.

Editorial Services of New England
126 Prospect Street
Cambridge, MA 02139

Provide temporary & permanent personnel for writing, editing, proofreading, etc.

Intermission Temporary Personnel Agency
505 Fifth Avenue
New York, NY 10017

Place Temporary office, field & editorial personnel.

Lynne Palmer Executive Recruitment
14 E. 60 Street
New York, NY 10022

Accept personnel in all areas & levels of publishing from senior executives to junior assistants, all areas of publishing.

Personnel Pool Inc.
Temporary Personnel Services
227 E. 45 Street, 11th Floor
New York, NY 10017

Place permanent & temporary personnel in clerical, word processing, editorial, etc.

Phone-a-Writer
One Fresenius Road
Westport, CT 06880

*Supply freelance writers for short-term
assignments for books, direct mail
packages, advertisements, brochures,
newsletters, technical manuals, speeches,
business & financial reports, etc.*

Professional Assignments
31 E. 32 Street, Suite 1200
New York, NY 10016

*Recruit full-time and freelance in all areas
of book and magazine publishing.*

SOCIETIES

American Society of Indexers
1700 N.W. 18 Street
Washington, DC 20009

*Provide educational programs for indexing
field. 800 members nationwide.*

Association of Desk Top Publishers
Box 881667
San Diego, CA 92108

*International trade association serving
needs of desk top publishers.*

**The Authors & Artists Resource
Center**
4001 E. Fort Lowell Road
Tuscon, AZ 85712

Serves writers, illustrators & photographers.

Bibliographical Society of America
Box 397, Grand Central Station
New York, NY 10063

*Sponsors short-term fellowships for
bibliographic projects.*

**Book Publicists of Southern
California**
6464 Sunset Blvd. Rm. 580
Hollywood, CA 90028

Promotion of books & authors.

The Children's Book Council
568 Broadway
New York, NY 10012

*Publish reading promotion display &
informational materials.*

**Copywriters Council of America
Freelance**
Bldg 102, LMP-91
Middle Island, NY 11953

*Professional organization of over 500
freelance direct-response advertising
copywriters & consultants.*

Editorial Freelancers Association
36 E. 23 Street, Room 9R
New York, NY 10010

*A professional association of freelance
writers, editors, proofreaders, indexers,
production specialists, researchers &
translators with over 900 members.*

Freelance Editorial Association
Box 835
Cambridge, MA 02238

*Organization for editorial freelancers,
including editors, writers, proofreaders,
indexers, project managers, researchers &
translators.*

APPENDIX 5

PARTIAL LISTING OF SOME
SCHOOLS AND COURSES

Courses in all facets of publishing can help you to better understand the material you will be proofreading, editing, and/or writing — you can never have too much knowledge, especially of subjects in which you are interested. While you are looking for work in these fields, you may want to consider taking courses such as the ones offered below to expand your knowledge and greatly enhance your "employability" in the publishing world.

Remember, this is by no means an exhaustive list — in fact, we included it only to give you some idea of the types of courses available. If none of the ones we list is sufficiently close to where you live, use this information to check up on schools and colleges in your own area until you find what you need locally.

California   **Also See Editorial Experts** under Virginia listings.

Stanford Publishing Course at Stanford University, Stanford Alumni Association, Bowman House, Stanford, CA 94305, (415) 725-1083.

University of California Extension Certificate Program in Publishing, 2223 Fulton Street, Berkeley, CA 94720, (415) 642-4231.

Courses in all major areas of publishing: editorial, marketing, management, production & design.

University of Southern California, Professional Writing Program, Waite Phillips Hall, Rm 404, Los Angeles, CA 90089-0031, (213) 740-2311.

Master's program in professional writing.

Colorado   **University of Denver Publishing Institute**, Dept. of Mass Communications, 2075 S. University Blvd.-D-114, Denver, CO 80210, (303) 871-2570.

Four-week summer institute on all phases of book publishing.

Connecticut   **The Book Manufacturers Institute (BMI)**, 111 Prospect Street, Stamford, CT 06901, (203) 324-9670.

BMI Book Manufacturing Seminar for Publishers

Florida   **Rene Gnam Consultation Corp.**, Box 3877, Holiday, FL 34690, (813) 938-1555. Book trade and graphic arts courses.

Hawaii   **University of Hawaii at Manoa, Writing Program**, 1733 Donaahho Road, Honolulu, HI 96822, (808) 948-8111.

Campus writing workshop.

Illinois   **Dynamic Graphics Educational Foundation**, Subs of Dynamic Graphics Inc., 6000 N. Forest Park Dr., Peoria, IL 61614, (309) 688-8866.

Basic Layout & Pasteup Techniques; Production Methods; Troubleshooting Offset Production; Color in Design & Reproduction; Paper & the Printed Image; Evaluating Computer Graphics; Layout & Design Techniques with a Computer Graphics Workstation; Step-by-Step Design Methods; Marker Techniques; Airbrush Illustration Techniques; Advanced Illustration; Designing the Newsletter; Publication Design; Typography in Design; Designing for Desktop Publishing.

Also See Editorial Experts under Virginia listings.

University of Chicago, Continuing Education Programs, 5835 Kimbark Avenue, Chicago, IL 60637, (312) 702-1722.

Courses in book editing, design, production, marketing and management for beginners & professionals.

University of Illinois at Chicago, Program for Writers, Dept. of English, Box 4348, Chicago, IL 60680, (312) 413-2200.

University of Illinois, Dept. of Journalism, 119 Gregory Hall, 810 S. Wright Street, Urbana, IL 61801, (217) 333-0709.

Courses: Magazine Article Writing, Magazine Editing.

<u>Iowa</u>	**University of Iowa, Writing Program**, Dept. of English, Iowa City, IA 52242, (319) 353-3976.

<u>Massachusetts</u>

Massachusetts College of Art, Workshop on Writing Children's Books, Continuing Education Department, 621 Huntington Avenue, Boston, MA 02115 (617) 731-0275.

Evening classes.

Radcliffe College/Harvard University, Radcliffe Publishing Procedures Course, 6 Ash Street, Cambridge, MA 02138, (617) 495-8678.

Course covers all aspects of book & magazine publishing.

Also See Editorial Experts under Virginia listings.

<u>Mississippi</u>	**University of Southern Mississippi, Center for Writers**, Dept. of English, Box 5144, Southern Sta., Hattiesburg, MS 39406, (601) 266-4321.

Undergraduate and graduate courses in fiction and poetry writing.

<u>New York</u>	**Association of the Graphic Arts, Graphic Arts Evening Educational Programs**, 5 Penn Plaza, New York, NY 10001 (212) 279-2100

Introduction to Printing and Printing Processes; Paper for the Graphic Arts; Binding: Production, Techniques & Impositions; Color Litho Reproduction, Principles & Techniques; Preparing Art for Printing; Modern Book Publishing/Production; Estimating Printing; Fundamentals of Printing Production; Elements of Offset Lithography; Computer Typography; Dynamics of Graphic Art Sales; Proofreading & Copy Editing; Electronic Scanning; Calligraphy; Printing Inks for the Graphic Arts; Form Design; Introduction to Business Forms; Electronic Manuscript Prep; Principles of Typography; Graphic Design; Fundamentals of Computers for the Graphic Arts; Font Identification

City University of New York, Graduate Center, Education in Publishing Program, 25 W. 43rd Street, Suite 300, New York, NY 10036, (212) 642-2910.

Children's Book Editing Workshop; Advanced Children's Book Editing Workshop; Copy Editing & Proofreading Workshop; Marketing of Specialized, Professional & Scholarly Books; Marketing & Sales for the Non-Specialist; Direct Mail Marketing of Books; Promotional Writing Workshop; The Economics of Publishing: Finance for the Non-Specialist; Production for the Non-Specialist; Book Publishing & the Law; Book Design Workshop; Managing People & Time in Publishing; Selling; Subsidiary Rights; Trade Book Editing Workshop; Paperback Publishing; Textbook Publishing; International Publishing; Line Editing Workshop; Marketing for Editors Workshop; The Profession of Literary Agent.

Columbia University, School of the Arts, Writing Division, 404 Dodge, New York, NY 10027, (212) 280-4391.

Two-year course leading to the MFA degrees. Seminars & workshops in poetry, fiction, nonfiction & translation.

Graphic Artists Guild, 11 W. 20th Street, 8th Floor, New York, NY 10011, (212) 463-7730.

Business workshops & seminars for artists.

Hofstra University, English Dept., 1000 Fulton Avenue, Hempstead, NY 11550 (516) 560-6600.

Undergraduate courses in all phases of publishing & for all types of writing.

Mystery Writers of America Inc., 236 W. 27th Street, New York, NY 10001, (212) 255-7005.

Mystery writing workshops in short story, private eye, young adult, romantic-suspense.

New York City Technical College, Center for Advertising, Printing & Publishing, 300 Jay Street, Brooklyn, NY 11201, (718) 643-3222.

New York University, Center for Publishing, School of Continuing Education, 48 Cooper Square, New York, NY 10003, (212) 998-7215.

Publishing and writing courses include: Introduction to Book Publishing; Book Editing; Copy Editing & Proofreading; Permissions & Subsidiary Rights; Trade Book Marketing; Book Production & Manufacturing; Basic Book Design; Freelance Book Indexing; Career Paths in Publishing.

Summer Institute in Book & Magazine Publishing: A 6-week residential program for recent college graduates entering the publishing industry. Two 3-week modules covering many aspects of the industry; assistance in job placement.

Parsons School of Design, Div. of The New School, 2 W. 13th Street, New York, NY 10011, (212) 229-8933.

Comprehensive graphic & advertising design courses and advanced courses appropriate for book design.

School of Visual Arts, 209 E. 23rd Street, New York, NY 10010, (212) 679-7350 or (212) 683-0600.

Book Illustration & Children's Book Writing & Illustration; Agency Skills; Cartooning; Public Relations; Business Writing; Copywriting.

Syracuse University, SI Newhouse School of Public Communications, Syracuse, NY 13244-2100 (315) 443-2301.

Undergraduate courses in advertising, public relations; all aspects of communications.

Ohio   **Writer's Digest School**, Div. of F&W Publications Inc., 1507 Dana Avenue, Cincinnati, OH 45207, (800) 759-0963; (513) 531-2222.

Courses in magazine article writing, short story writing, novel writing & the elements of effective writing. Courses are by correspondence; student has two years to complete.

Pennsylvania **The Publishing Institute**, The University of Pennsylvania, 3808 Walnut Street, Philadelphia, PA 19104-6136, (215) 898-6479.

Extensive overview of the book publishing industry, including editing and production. For people considering a career change, and/or for writers and recent college grads.

University of Pennsylvania, Publishing Institute, College of General Studies, 3808 Walnut Street, Philadelphia, PA 19104-6136, (215) 898-6493.

Course offers overview of the book publishing industry, from acquisition of manuscripts to editing and production, etc. Certificate of completion offered.

Texas **University of Houston - University Park, Writing Program**, Dept. of English, Houston, TX 77004, (713) 749-3640.

Offers MA or PhD in creative writing.

University of Texas at Austin, Writing Program, Dept. of English, Austin, TX 78712, (512) 471-5132.

A full range of poetry & fiction writing courses with concentration in creative writing.

University of Texas at El Paso, Writing Program, Dept. of English, El Paso, TX 79968, (915) 747-5731.

Courses: Intro to Creative Writing; Non-Fiction Writing; Commercial Fiction; Screen & TV Writing; Special Problems in Writing.

Virginia **Editorial Experts Inc.**, 85 S. Bragg St., Suite 400, Alexandria, VA 22312-2731, (703) 683-0683.

Basic through advanced workshops in publication skills, including grammar, writing, editing, proofreading, production, publications management, proposal preparation, indexing & newsletters. Professional workshops currently offered in Washington, Boston, Chicago & San Francisco.

Washington   **Copyright Information Services**, Box 1460-A, Friday Harbor, WA 98250 (206) 378-5128.

Courses on applications of the copyrights law for educators, librarians, authors, artists, other creators & users of copyrighted works.

Washington   **See Editorial Experts** under Virginia listings.

Washington DC

George Washington University, Center for Career Education & Workshops, Publication Specialist Program, 801 22nd Street NW, Suite T-409, Washington, DC 20052, (202) 994-7273.

Basic & advanced courses in editing, writing, design, production, marketing, business & management of publications. 8-week evening courses; include material on all aspects of the publishing industry from editing to marketing.

Howard University Press Book Publishing Institute, 2900 Van Ness Street NW, Washington, DC 20008 (202) 806-8468.

Five-week course provides basic overview of the book publishing industry. Certificates awarded upon completion of course.

Wisconsin   **University of Wisconsin - Madison Communications Programs**, 214 Lowell Hall, 610 Langdon St., Madison, WI 53703, (608) 262-3982.

Courses: Brochure Design Workshop; Newsletter Workshop; Copyright Workshop; Writing for Magazines; Writing to Publish; Writing Advertising Copy That Sells; Report Writing Workshop; Newswriting; Article Writing for Fun & Profit; Humor Writing; Food & Nutrition Writing; Sports Writing; Publicity Techniques.

APPENDIX 6

PARTIAL LISTING OF SOME PUBLISHERS

BY STATE

The following list is included to provide you with more opportunities to follow up for yourself. We have included only a few of the literally thousands of publishers nationwide. *Please remember that being included in this listing does not mean the company is seeking or even uses freelance help.* You should WRITE TO (not phone) companies that interest you, including either a self-addressed, stamped envelope or a stamped postcard for their reply. Again, please **NEVER** telephone — a polite letter of inquiry along with the courtesy of a postage-paid reply envelope will project a professional image.

ALABAMA

Books Americana Inc
Federal Personnel Management Institute
 Inc
Gryphon Editions Ltd
Menasha Ridge Press
Oxmoor House Inc
Religious Education Press
Summa Publications Inc
University of Alabama Press

ARIZONA

American Federation of Astrologers
Aztex Corp
The Body Press
Communication Skill Builders Inc
CYMA/McGraw-Hill
Falcon Press
Gorsuch Scarisbrick Publishers
HP Books
Northland Press
The Oryx Press
Phoenix Books Publishers
The University of Arizona Press
Westernlore Press
Word Beat Press

ARKANSAS

August House Inc, Publishers
ESP Inc

Rose Publishing Co Inc
The University of Arkansas Press

CALIFORNIA

Abbot, Foster & Hauserman Co
Academic Therapy Publications
Advocacy Press
Alchemy Books
Andersons Publications
The Arion Press
Astronomical Society of The Pacific
Bedford Press
The Benjamin-Cummings Publishing Co
Blue Dolphin Publishing Inc
The Boxwood Press
Robert Briggs Associates
Business Books Marketing Group
California State University Press
Career Publishing Inc
Celestial Arts
China Books & Periodicals Inc
The Arthur H Clark Co
College-Hill Press
Craftsman Book Co
Creative Teaching Press Inc
Crossroads Press
John Daniel, Publisher
De Vorss & Co
Dustbooks
ETC Publications
J Flores Publications
Forman Publishing Inc
Freeman, Cooper & Co

Gem Guides Book Co
The Green Tiger Press
Guinness Productions Inc
Hay House Inc
Heridonius Foundation
Holden Day Inc
Hope Publishing House
ICS Press
Impact Publishers Inc
Interurban Press
Jalmar Press Inc
Jones Medical Publications
Kalimat Press
The Knapp Press
David S Lake Publishers
The Lapis Press
Lexikos
Life Action Press
Lonely Planet Publications
McGraw-Hill Training Systems
Mayfield Publishing Co
R & E Miles Publishers
Monday Morning Books Inc
Network Publications
Nolo Press
Oak Tree Publications Inc
Ortho Information Services
Padre Productions
Parallax Press
Peninsula Publishing
Prima Publishing & Communications
QED Press
Ramparts Press Inc
Regal Books
Ross Books
Royal House Publishing Co Inc
San Francisco Press Inc
Shameless Hussy Press
Snow Lion Graphics
The Soyfoods Center
Squarebooks Inc
Strawberry Hill Press
Sunset Books
SysteMetrics/McGraw-Hill
Theosophical Book Association for the
    Blind Inc
Travel Keys
Univelt Inc
University of California Press
Valley of the Sun Publishing Co
VHW Publishing
Vortex Communications Inc
Western Marine Enterprises Inc
Whatever Publishing Inc

Wilshire Book Co
Wizards Bookshelf
Woodbridge Press Publishing Co

COLORADO

Accent Books
Blue Mountain Arts Inc
Bookmakers Guild Inc
Chidvilas Foundation Inc
Chockstone Press Inc
Colorado Associated University Press
Colorado School of Mines Press
Communication Creativity About
    Books Inc
Cordillera Press Inc
Filter Press
Fulcrum Inc
Geological Society of America (GSA)
Johnson Books
Lace Publications
Libraries Unlimited Inc
Love Publishing Co
Meriwether Publishing Ltd/Contemporary
    Drama Service
NavPress
The Old Army Press
Paladin Press
Pruett Publishing Co
Renaissance House Publishers
Lynne Rienner Publishers Inc
Fred B Rothman & Co
Shepard's/McGraw-Hill
Westcliffe Publishers Inc
Westview Press Inc
Wiley Law Publications

CONNECTICUT

Appleton & Lange
Architectural Book Publishing Co Inc
BackPax International Ltd
Bison Books Corp
Black Swan Books Ltd
Business & Legal Reports
Chatham Press
Cortina Learning International Inc
Creative Learning Press Inc
Curbstone Press
Devin-Adair Publishers Inc
The Dushkin Publishing Group Inc
East Rock Press Inc

East Rock Press Inc
Field Publications
Folio Pubilishing Corp
Food & Nutrition Press Inc
Foreign Intelligence Press
The C R Gibson Co
Grey House Publishing Inc
Grolier Inc
Grolier TeleMarketing Inc
Lawrence Hill & Co Publishers Inc
HRAF Press
Hyperion Press Inc
International Resource Development Inc
International Universities Press Inc
JAI Press Inc
The Jargon Society
Keats Publishing Inc
Knights Press
Kumarian Press Inc
Market Data Retrieval Inc
The Meckler Corp
Modern Books & Crafts Inc
Morehouse-Barlow Co Inc
Joshua Morris Publishing Inc
Mustang Publishing Co Inc
Mystic Seaport Museum
New Haven Editorial Office
Ox Bow Press
Pendulum Press Inc
Peregrine Press
Prayer Book Press Inc
The Shoe String Press Inc
The Southfarm Press
Special Learning Corp
Sphinx Press Inc
The Taunton Press
Twenty-Third Publications Inc
US Games Systems Inc
Verbatim Books
Wesleyan University Press
Yale University Press

DELAWARE

Juan de la Cuesta-Hispanic Monographs
Michael Glazier Inc
Middle Atlantic Press
Scholarly Resources Inc
University of Delaware Press

DISTRICT OF COLUMBIA

Acropolis Books Ltd
American Association for the
    Advancement of Science (AAAS)
American Chemical Society
American Council on Education
American Enterprise Insititute for Public
    Policy Research
American Psychiatric Press Inc
The Alexander Graham Bell Association
    for the Deaf Inc
BNA Books
The Brookings Institution
The Catholic University of America Press
Cato Institute
Center for Applied Linguistics
Child Welfare League of America Inc
    (CWLA)
Columbia Books Inc
Computer Society Press of the IEEE
Congressional Quarterly Inc
The Conservation Foundation
Ethics & Public Policy Center
Gallaudet Unversity Press
Georgetown Unversity Press
HBJ, Washington, DC:
Howard Unversity Press
Institute for International Economics
Institute for Policy Studies
International Labour Office
International Monetary Fund (IMF)
Island Press
McGraw-Hill Continuing Education
    Center
The Mathematical Association of America
National Academy Press
National Aeronautics & Space
    Administration (NASA)
National Education Association (NEA)
National Geographic Society
Organization for Economic Cooperation
    & Development
Organization of American States
Preservation Press
Production Division
Public Affairs Press
Regnery Gateway Inc
Resources for the Future
Smithsonian Institution Press
Special Libraries Association (SLA)
Starrhill Press
Stone Wall Press Inc
The Taft Group

Three Continents Press
U S Government Printing Office
The Urban Institute Press
The Washington Institute Press
Women's Legal Defense Fund
World Bank
Worldwatch Institute

FLORIDA

Atlantis Publishing Co
Banyan Books Inc
CRC Press Inc
Ediciones Universal
Editorial Caribe
Editorial Concepts Inc
Frederick Fell Publishers Inc
Fiesta Publishing Corp
Flora & Fauna Publications
HBJ, Orlando
Health Communications Inc
Holt, Rinehart & Winston Inc
The International Society of Dramatists
B Klein Publications
R E Krieger Publishing Co Inc
Learning Publications Inc
Loiry Publishing House
The Naiad Press Inc
The Penkevill Publishing Co
The Pickering Press
Pineapple Press Inc
Professional Resource Exchange Inc
Rainbow Books/Betty Wright
Success Advertising & Publishing
Surfside Publishing Inc
Triad Publishing Co Inc
UNIFO Publishers Ltd
The University of Florida Libraries
University Presses of Florida
US Directory Service
Van Arsdales Video Travel Guides
Wake-Brook House

GEORGIA

Clarity Press
The Fairmont Press Inc
Georgia State University, College of
    Business Administration, Business
    Publishing Division
Humanics Ltd
John Knox Press

Larlin Corp
Mercer University Press
Mockingbird Books
Oddo Publishing Inc
Peachtree Publishers Ltd
Scholars Press
University of Georgia Press

IDAHO

Ahsahta Press
The Caxton Printers Ltd
Pacific Press Publishing Association
University of Idaho Press

ILLINOIS

Academy Chicago Publishers
American Hospital Publishing Inc
American Library Association (ALA)
Ares Publishers Inc
Art Institute of Chicago
Baha'i Publishing Trust
Bonus Books Inc
Center for Urban Policy
The Child's World Inc
Coach House Press Inc
Compton's Learning Co
Crain Books/NTC Business Books
Harlan Davidson Inc
The Dorsey Press
The Dramatic Publishing Co
Encyclopedia Britannica Educational
    Corp
Glencoe Publishing Co/Bennett &
    McKnight
Goodheart-Willcox Co
Institute of Modern Languages
Interpharm Press Inc
Richard D Irwin Inc
Kazi Publications
Leisure Press
Lion Publishing Corp
Longman Financial Services Publishing
McDougal, Littell & Co
Meyer Stone Books
The Mobium Press
Thomas More Press
National Register Publishing Co
Nelson-Hall Publishers
Northwestern University Press

Open Court Publishing Co
Planners Press
Prestressed Concrete Institute
Quintessence Publishing Co Inc
Research Press
St James Press
Scripture Press Publications Inc
Society For Visual Education Inc
SPSS Inc
Standard Educational Corp
Sherwood Sugden & Co
Templegate Publishers
Charles C Thomas, Publisher
Turnbull & Willoughby Publishers
United Educators Inc
Unversity O Illinois Press
Victor Books
Wallace-Homestead Book Co
Albert Whitman & Co
Year Book Medical Publishers

INDIANA

Accelerated Development Inc
And Books
Ave Maria Press
Benchmark Press Inc
Cram Cassettes
Cross Cultural Publications Inc
Dean Aster Publishing Co
Diamond Communications Inc
Friends United Press
Hackett Publishing Co Inc
Indiana Unversity Press
Knoll Publishing Co Inc
Liberty Fund Inc
Our Sunday Visitor Publishing
Phi Delta Kappa Educational Foundation
Purdue University Press
Que Corp
Howard W Sams & Co Inc, Publishers
University of Notre Dame Press

IOWA

Ad-Lib Publications
Better Homes & Gardens Book
Wm C Brown Group
Iowa State University Press
Kendall/Hunt Publishing Co
Meredith Corp

University of Iowa Press
World Bible Publishers Inc

KANSAS

Coronado Press Inc
Learning Resources Network (LRN)
MA/AH Publishing
Sunflower University Press
University Press of Kansas
Veterinary Medicine Publishing

KENTUCKY

American Printing House for the Blind
    Inc
Collector Books
French Forum Publishers Inc
Gnomon Press
The University Press of Kentucky

LOUISIANA

Anchorage Press Inc
Bale Books
Louisiana State University Press
Pelican Publishing Co Inc

MAINE

Cay-Bel Publishing Co
Cobblesmith
DeLorme Mapping Co
Dog Ear Press
Down East Books
Gannett Books
Harpswell Press
Intercultural Press Inc
International Marine Publishing
Northwoods Press
Puckerbrush Press
Lance Tapley, Publisher
TBW Books Inc
Thorndike Press
J Weston Walch Publisher
Samuel Weiser Inc

MARYLAND

Acheron Press
ARCsoft Publishers
Aspen Publishers Inc
Joseph J Binns Publisher
Paul H Brookes Publishing Co
Christian Classics Inc
Computer Science Press Inc
The Consultant's Library
Dryad Press
Family Line Publications
Government Institutes Inc
Half Halt Press
International Library-Book Publishers Inc
Kar-Ben Copies Inc
Lomond Publications Inc
Madison Books
National Association of the Deaf
The Nautical & Aviation Publishing Co of
    America Inc
Ottenheimer Publishers Inc
Review & Herald Publishing Association
Seven Locks Press Inc
Stemmer House Publishers Inc
Tidewater Publishers
University Press of America Inc
Urban & Schwarzenberg Inc
Woodbine House

MASSACHUSETTS

Bob Adams Inc
Affirmation Books
Allen & Unwin Inc
Alyson Publication
Applewood Books Inc
Artech House Inc
Theodore Audel & Co
Bankers Publishing Co
Robert Bentley Inc
Berkshire Traveller Press
Blackwell Scientific Publications Inc
Boyd & Freser Publishing Co
Braille Inc
Charles T Branford Co
Charles River Books
The Collamore Press
John Curley & Associates Inc
Dante University of America Press Inc
Davis Publications Inc (MA)
Educators Publishing Service Inc
Federal Research Press

Financial Publishing Co
Ginn & Co
David R Godine, Publisher Inc
Hadronic Press Inc
Harvard Business School Press
Heinle & Heinle Publishers Inc
Houghton Mifflin Co
IHRDC (International Human Resources
    Development Corp)
Jones & Bartlett Publishers Inc
Kluwer Academic Publishers
Learning Center Books
Mastery Education
Merriam-Webster Inc
Mills & Sanderson Publishers
National Braille Press
New York Graphic Society Books
Oelgeschlager, Gunn & Hain Inc,
    Publishers
Paraclete Press
Peabody Museum Publications
Pittenbruach Press
Practice Management Associates Ltd
PSG Publishing Co Inc
QED Information Sciences Inc
Quinlan Press
Routledge & Kegan Paul Inc
Salem House Publishers Ltd
Schenkman Books Inc
Sigo Press
Peter Smith Publisher Inc
University of Massachusetts Press
Watson Publishing International
The Writer Inc

MICHIGAN

Ardis Publishers
Avery Color Studios
Baker Book House
Christian Schools International
Cistercian Publications Inc
Wm B Eerdmans Publishing Co
The Evangelical Literature League
The Fideler Co
Gale Research Co
Gollehon Press Inc
Harbor House Publishers
Health Administration Press
Hillsdales College
Home Planners Inc
Information Coordinators Inc
International Book Centre

Japanese Technical Information Service
Karoma Publishers Inc
Kinseeker Publications
Cregel Publications
Lewis Publishers Inc
Lotus Press Inc
Masters Press
Michigan State University Press
Mott Media Inc Publishers
Out-of-Print Books On Demand
Phanes Press
The Pierian Press
Prakken Publications Inc
Reference Publications Inc
Servant Publications
UMI Research Press
University Microfilms International
The University of Michigan Press
Wayne State University Press
Wellness Publications
Wilderness Adventure Books Inc
Zondervan Publishing House

MINNESOTA

Augsburg Publishing House
Baker Street Productions Ltd
Bethany House Publishers
Burgess International Group Inc
Carolrhoda Books Inc
Coffee House Press
CompCare Publishers
Creative Education Inc
Crestwood House Inc
Data Research Inc
Cy Decosse Inc
T S Denison & Co Inc
Diabetes Center Inc
Dillon Press Inc
EMC Corp
EMS McGraw-Hill
Free Spirit Publishing Co
Graywolf Press
Greenhaven Press Inc
Guild Press
Hazelden Publishing
IWP Publishing Inc
Lerner publications Co
The Liturgical Press
Llewellyn Publications
Meadowbrook Press Inc
Milkweed Editions
Minnesota Historical Society Press

Paradon Publishing Co
Redpath Press
Saint Mary's Press
Soldier Creek Press
Thompson & Co Inc
University of Minnesota Press
West Publishing Co
Whole Person Associates Inc

MISSISSIPPI

University Press of Mississippi

MISSOURI

Andrews, McMeel & Parker
The Catholic Health Association of the
    United States
CBP Press
College Press Publishing Co
Fireside Books
Gospel Publishing House
Warren H Green Inc
Herald House
Ishiyaku EuroAmerica Inc
Liguori Publications
C V Mosby Co
Multi-Media Publishing Inc
Pentecostal Publishing House
The Sporting News Publishing Co
Test Corp of America
University of Missouri Press

MONTANA

Falcon Press Publishing Co Inc
Mountain Press Publishing Co

NEBRASKA

Cliff Notes Inc
Media Productions & Marketing Inc
University of Nebraska Press

NEVADA

Iris I O Publishing
KC Publications
University of Nevada Press

NEW HAMPSHIRE

William L Bauhan, Publisher
Boynton/Cook Publishers Inc
Consultants News
Ediciones del Norte
Entelek
The Golden Quill Press
Heinemann Educational Books Inc
Longwood Publishing Group Inc
New Hampshire Publishing Co
Phoenix Publishing
Stillpoint Publishing
University Press of New England

NEW JERSEY

Ablex Publishing Corp
American School of Classical Studies,
    Publications
Jason Aronson Inc
Barbour & Co Inc
Behrman House Inc
Birch Tree Group Ltd
Bureau of Business Practice
Castle Books Inc
Chartwell Books Inc
Citadel Press
Crane Publishing Co
The Darwin Press Inc
Down The Shore Publishing
Educational Testing Service
Lawrence Erlbaum Assocaites Inc
Folger Books
Hammond Inc
Humana Press
Hunter Publishing Inc
Augustus M Kelley, Publishers
Lincoln Springs Press
Loizeaux Brothers Inc
The Main Street Press
New Century Education Corp
New Horizon Press
Jerome S Ozer Publisher Inc
Parker Publishing Co
Peterson's Guides Inc
Prentice Hall, Prentice Hall Press
Princeton Architectural Press
Princeton University Press
Fleming H Revell Co
Rowman & Littlefield, Publishers
Salem Press Inc

Scarecrow Press Inc
Sharon Publications Inc
Simon & Schuster International Group
Simon & Schuster School Group
Slack Inc
Lyle Stuart Inc
TFH Publications Inc
Troll Associates
University Books Inc
Winchester Press

NEW MEXICO

Amador Publishers
American Classical College Press
Bear & Co Inc
Institute for Economic & Financial
    Research
Institute for Economic & Political World
    Strategic Studies
The Lightning Tree
John Muir Publications Inc
Museum of New Mexico Press
The Rio Grande Press Inc
Sun Publishing Co
The Sunstone Press
University of New Mexico Press

NEW YORK

A B Cowles Co/Brooke-House
ACA Books
Adler Publishing Co
Agathon Press Inc
Almar Press
The American Alpine Club
American Institute of Chemical Engineers
American Life Books
American Society of Civil Engineers
AMS Press Inc
Apollo Book
Arco Publishing Co
Asher-Gallant Press
Associated Faculty Press Inc
The Atlantic Monthly Press
Aurora Press
Ball-Stick-Bird Publications Inc
Lilian Barber Press Inc
Basic Books Inc, Publishers
Beech Tree Books
Matthew Bender & Co Inc
Berlitz Publications Inc

Bloch Publishing Co Inc
Thomas Bouregy & Co Inc
George Braziller Inc
Buckley-Little Book Catalogue Co Inc
Aristide D Caratzas, Publisher
Carroll & Graf Publishers Inc
Chanticleer Press Inc
Cherry Lane Books
Clarion Books
College Entrance Examination Board
Consumer Reports Books
Council on Foreign Relations Inc
Critic's Choice Paperbacks/Lorevan
    Publishing Inc
Custombook Inc
Aldine de Gruyter
Dell Publishing Co
Direct Marketing Association Inc (DMA)
Dorset Press
Dramatists Play Service Inc
The Ecco Press
Epimetheus Press Inc
Fairchild Books & Visuals
Howard Fertig Inc, Publisher
Fleet Press Corp
The Foundation Center
Free Press
Eleanor Friede Books Inc
Fromm International Publishing Corp
Galison Books
Bernard Geis Associates Inc
Glanville Publishers Inc
Golden Press-Books for Adults
Gower Medical Publishing Ltd
Grosset & Dunlap Inc
Gull Books
Harlequin Enterprises, Inc.
Hanging Loose Press
The Harrington Park Press Inc
The Haworth Press Inc
The Hearst Trade Book Group
Hemisphere Publishing Corp
Hippocrene Books Inc
Henry Holt & Co
Human Sciences Press Inc
Igaku-Shoin Medical Publishers Inc
Institute of International Education
Jane's Publishing Inc
S Darger AG
Alfred A Knopf Inc
Kraus International Publications
Larimi Communications Associates Ltd
Seymour Lawrence Inc
Lebhar-Friedman Books

Lieber-Atherton Inc
Living Flame Press
Lothrop, Lee & Shepard Books
McGraw-Hill Inc
McPherson & Co
Media Projects Inc
Methuen Inc
Modern Language Association of
    America (MLA)
The Moretus Press Inc
Moyer Bell Ltd
National Learning Corp
New City Press
New Readers Press
Newbury House Publishers Inc
W W Norton & Co Inc
Optimization Software Inc, Publications
    Division
The Overlook Press
Pantheon Books Inc
PBC International Inc
Pergamon Press Inc
Peter Pauper Press Inc
The Pilgrim Press/United Church Press
The Plough Publishing House
Carkson N Potter Inc
Prometheus Books
The Putnam Publishing Group Inc
Rawson Associates
Reading Rainbow Gazette Inc
Richardson & Steirman Book Publishers
The Rosen Publishing Group Inc
Russell Sage Foundation
The Salesman's Guide Inc
Scholars' Facsimiles & Reprints
Scientific American Books
Sepher-Hermon Press Inc
Shengold Publishers Inc
Simon & Schuster Inc
Robert Speller & Sons, Publishers Inc
Springer-Verlag New York Inc
Stein & Day Publishers
Stravon Educational Press
Tahrike Tarsile Qur'an Inc
Thames & Hudson Inc
Thunder's Mouth Press Inc
Tor Books
Tuffy Books Inc
United Nations
Unlimited Publishing Co
VCH Publishers Inc
Warner Books Inc
Weidenfeld & Nicolson
Whitston Publishing Co

198

Windsor Books
World Policy Institute
Youth Education Systems

NORTH CAROLINA

Algonquin Books of Chapel Hill
Appalachian Consortium Press
John F Blair, Publisher
Carolina Academic Press
Carolina Biological Supply Co
Duke University Press
Gallopade Publishing Group
Instrument Society of America
The Labyrinth Press
McFarland & Co Inc, Publishers
Omni Learning Institute
Unicorn Press Inc
The University of North Carolina Press
Wake Forest University Press

OHIO

Advocate Publishing Group
Alpha Publishing Co
Anderson Publishing Co
Antioch Publishing Co
Ariel Press
Banks-Baldwin Law Publishing Co
Battelle Press
Bits Press
Cleveland State University Poetry Center
Clovernook Printing House for the Blind
Columbus Publishing Co
The Corinthian Press
CSS of Ohio
Daring Publishing Group
Kent State University Press
The McDonald & Woodward Publishing Co
Merrill Publishing Co
Modern Curriculum Press Inc
Morningside Bookshop
North Light Publishers
Ohio State University Press
Ohio University Press
Pflaum Press
The Popular Press
Publishing Horizons Inc
St Anthony Messenger Press
Scott Publishing Co
Slavica Publishers Inc

South-Western Publishing Co
ST Publications Book Division
Standard Publishing
Writer's Digest Books
Zaner-Bloser Inc

OKLAHOMA

Council Oak Books Ltd
EDC Publishing
Harrison House Publishers
McGraw-Hill School Division
PennWell Books
Pueblo Publishing Press
University of Oklahoma Press

OREGON

Beautiful America Publishing Co
Binford & Mort
Circa Press
Dormac Inc
Graphic Arts Center Publishing Co
Harvest House Publishers Inc
Maverick Publications
Metamorphouse Press Inc
Multnomah Press
National Book Co
Oregon Historical Society Press
Oregon State University Press
Quicksilver Productions
SOS Publishing
Timber Press Inc

PENNSYLVANIA

Alpha Publications Inc
American Law Institute-American Bar
   Association Committee on
   Continuing Professional Education
American Poetry & Literature Press
ASTM
John Benjamins North America Inc
Camino Books
Chilton Book Co
F A Davis Co
Dufour Editions Inc
Fisher's Word Inc
Foreign Policy Research Institute
The Franklin Library
Graphic Arts Technical Foundation

Harwal Publishing Co
Himalayan Publishers
Institute for the Study of Human Issues
    (ISHI)
Jewish Publication Society
Lea & Febiger
J B Lippincott Co
Medical Manor Books
Morgan-Rand Publications Inc
New Society Publishers
Para Research Inc
Philadelphia Editorial Office
J Pohl Associates
Richboro Press
Running Press Book Publishers
W B Saunders Co
Seth Press Inc
Springhouse Corp
George F Stickley Co
Technomic Publishing Co Inc
Temple University Press
Underwood-Miller
University of Pittsburgh Press
Whitaker House

RHODE ISLAND

The Carroll Press
Jamestown Publishers
Janson Publications Inc
PAR Inc
Rhode Island Publications Society

SOUTH CAROLINA

Bob Jones University Press
Bruccoli Clark Layman Publishers
Camden House Inc
Reprint Co Publishers
Southern Historical Press Inc
University of South Carolina Press

SOUTH DAKOTA

Melius & Peterson, Publishing Inc

TENNESSEE

AASLH Press
Abingdon Press

Battery Press Inc
Broadman Press
Holman Bible Publishers
Ideals Publishing Corp
Incentive Publications Inc
Ion Books Inc
Memphis State University Press
Thomas Nelson Inc
Pathway Press
St Lukes Press
University of Tennessee Press
The Upper Room
Vanderbilt University Press
White Rose Press
Winston-Derek Publishers Inc
Wolgemuth & Hyatt Publishers Inc

TEXAS

ACU Press
American Atheist Press Inc
Arte Publico Press
Askon Publishing Co
Baptist Publishing House
Baylor University Press
The Blue Boar Press
Boy Scouts of America
Business Publications Inc
Butterworth Legal Publishers
Cap & Gown Press Inc
Casa Bautista de Publicaciones
Cinco Puntos Press
Creative Publishing Co
Dame Publications Inc
Steve Davis Publishing
DLM Teaching Resources
Eakin Press
Gulf Publishing Co, Book Div
Holt, Rinehart & Winston Inc School
    Division
Multi Media Arts
Pressworks Publishing Inc
PRO-ED
Radio Shack
Rice University Press
Rossel Books
Saybrook
Scholarly Publications
Southern Methodist University Press
Spring Publications Inc
State House Press
Steck-Vaughn Co

Summer Institute of Linquistics,
    Academic Publications
Sweet Publishing Co
Tabor Publishing
Taylor Publishing Co
Texas A & M University Press
Texas Christian Unversity Press
Texas Instruments Inc Information
    Publishing Center
Texas Monthly Press Inc
Texas Tech University Press
Texas Western Press
Trinity University Press
University of Texas Press
WindRiver Publishing Co
Word Inc
Wordware Publishing Inc

UTAH

Accelerated Indexing Systems Inc
Deseret Book Co
Dream Garden Press
Hascom Publishers Inc
Hawkes Publishing Inc
Horizon Publishers & Distributors Inc
Howe Brothers
Gibbs M Smith Inc
University of Utah Press
Utah State University Press
The Vanessa-Ann Collection
Woodland Books

VERMONT

Amana Books
Backcountry Publications Inc
Brookfield Publishing Co
Chelsea Green Publishing Co
The Countryman Press Inc
Paul S Eriksson, Publisher
Garden Way Publishing
Inner Traditions International Ltd
The Marlboro Press
Media Forum International Ltd
The New England Press Inc
Oliver Wight Ltd Publications Inc
Pro Lingua Associates
Seafarers Heritage Library
Thorsons Publishers Inc
Threshold Books
Trafalgar Square Publishers

Charles E Tuttle Co Inc
Waterfront Books
Williamson Publishing Co

VIRGINIA

ABBE Publishers Association of
    Washington DC
American Society for Training &
    Development (ASTD)
Association for Research &
    Enlightenment Inc (ARE)
Association of University Programs in
    Health Administration (AUPHA)
Betterway Publications Inc
Brunswick Publishing Co
Chadwyck-Healey Inc
The Colonial Williamsburg Foundation
Commonwealth Press Inc
Denlingers Publishers Ltd
The Donning Co/Publishers
EPM Publications Inc
Great Ocean Publishers
Grosvenor USA
Grunwald & Radcliff Publishers
Hero Books
Howell Press Inc
Inner Vision Publishing Co
Institute of Early American History &
    Culture
James River Press
Lintel
The Michie Co Law Publishing
National Council of Teachers of
    Mathematics
Octameron Associates
Thomasson-Grant Inc
Time-Life Books Inc
The University Press of Virginia

WASHINGTON

Aglow Publications
Alaska Northwest Publishing Co
Bilingual Books Inc
Copper Canyon Press
Copyright Information Services
Daisy Publishing Inc
Fjord Press
Hartley & Marks Inc
Lambert Gann Publishing Co
Madrona Publishers Inc

Mountaineers Books
Outdoor Empire Publishing Inc
Pacific Search Press
Parenting Press Inc
Peanut Butter Publishing
The Real Comet Press
Seal Press
Self-Counsel Press Inc
Signpost Books
Sovereignty Inc
SPIE, International Society for Optical
    Engineering
Starmont House Inc
University of Washington Press
Ye Galleon Press

WEST VIRGINIA

Palace Publishing

WISCONSIN

A-R Editions Inc
Aardvark/McGraw-HIll
American Society of Agronomy
Angel Press of Wisconsin
Arcadia Publications
Arkham House Publishers Inc
Caledonia Press
Educators Progress Service Inc
Family Service America
Kalmbach Publishing Co
Kitchen Sink Press Inc
Hal Leonard Books
Motorbooks International Publishers &
    Wholesalers Inc
Pleasant Co
Praxis Publications Inc
Raintree Publishers Inc
Science Tech Publishers
Sheffield Publishing Co
Stanton & Lee Publishers Inc
State Historical Society of Wisconson
Gareth Stevens Inc
TSR Inc
University of Wisconsin Press
Western Publishing Co Inc
Willow Creek Press Inc

WYOMING

UW Publications

APPENDIX 7

WRITING A READER'S REPORT

If you have never worked in this capacity before, you will want to give a publisher samples of your ability. Key elements that are important in making up a reader's report include:

1. **Where or what is the setting of the book?**

2. **What is the general theme?**

3. **Who are the major characters?**

4. **What are the major events in the manuscript?**

5. **What conflicts and interests do the major characters have?**

6. **How enjoyable was the book to you?**

7. **If you enjoyed it, why?**

8. **If you didn't enjoy the book, what are your reasons?**

9. **Would you recommend this book for others to read?**

10. **What type of person would this book appeal to?**

11. **Do you think that the book has sales potential?**

These questions are geared for fictional manuscripts, usually in the television and movie industries. Obviously, if you are reading an educational text, instruction manuals, etc., you would be looking for how informative the book is, rather than how entertaining.

SAMPLE FORM FOR READER'S REPORTS

READER'S REPORT

DATE: _____

TITLE OF BOOK:_____

AUTHOR: _____

READER'S NAME: _____

TYPE OF BOOK:

SETTING:

DESCRIPTION OF CONTENTS:

COMMENTS:

RECOMMENDATIONS:

APPENDIX 8

WRITER'S WORKSHOPS, CONFERENCES AND CLASSES

Authors who are just getting started do not have the support of publishing houses that established authors have, and they very often need assistance with their publications. Whether you are interested in copyediting, indexing, proofreading or reading books onto tapes, it may benefit you tremendously to attend or advertise at the conferences and workshops being held in your general area. One excellent idea is to stand outside the door at these conferences and workshops and hand out small flyers with your name, address and phone number, together with information about your services. You may also wish to approach teachers of regularly scheduled classes in order to pass your name along to the students. Use the following partial listing as a starting point, but also scan your local paper for notices about other workshops.

WHAT: ACT I CREATIVITY CENTER
WHEN: Year-round
WHERE: Lake of the Ozarks, MO
INFO: ACTS Institute Inc., 4550 Warwick Blvd., Apt. 1201-02, Kansas City, MO 64111, (816) 753-0208 or (314) 365-4404

WHAT: ANNUAL WRITERS' CONFERENCE
WHEN: Annually in May
WHERE: New York, NY
INFO: American Society of Journalists & Authors, 1501 Broadway, Suite 1907, New York, NY 10036

WHAT: ANNUAL BLACK WRITER'S CONFERENCE
WHEN: Last weekend in July
WHERE: Los Angeles, CA
INFO: Black Writers Workshop Committee, Box 43576, Los Angeles, CA 90043

WHAT: ANNUAL WORKSHOP
WHEN: June
WHERE: Atlanta, GA
INFO: Dixie Council of Authors & Journalists Inc., 2860 Evansdale Circle NE, Atlanta, GA 30340 (404) 939-1924

WHAT: ANNUAL WRITERS' CONFERENCE
WHEN: October
WHERE: Ocala, FL and other locations (get info)
INFO: Editor's Desk, 709 SE 52nd Avenue, Ocala, FL 32671

WHAT:	ANNUAL WRITERS' SEMINAR
WHEN:	Annually in January
WHERE:	Tucson, AZ
INFO:	The Society of Southwestern Authors (SSA), Box 41897, Tucson, AZ 85717, (602) 629-2809

WHAT:	ARKANSAS WRITERS' CONFERENCE
WHEN:	Annually in June
WHERE:	Little Rock, AR
INFO:	1115 Gillette Drive, Little Rock, AR 72207, (501) 225-0166

WHAT:	ASPEN WRITERS' CONFERENCE
WHEN:	Annual conference in July; weekly workshops; monthly readings
WHERE:	Aspen, CO
INFO:	Box 7726, Aspen, CO 81612, (303) 925-3122

WHAT:	THE AUTHORS & ARTISTS RESOURCE CENTER (TARC)
WHEN:	Year-round
WHERE:	Tucson, AZ
INFO:	4001 E. Fort Owell Road, Tucson, AZ 85712, (602) 325-4733

WHAT:	BROOKLYN WRITERS' CLUB
WHEN:	Third Saturday of each month
WHERE:	Brooklyn, NY
INFO:	Box 184, Bath Beach Station, Brooklyn, NY 11214, (718) 837-3484

WHAT:	BROOKLYN WRITERS' NETWORK WORKSHOPS
WHEN:	Twice monthly
WHERE:	Brooklyn, NY
INFO:	2509 Avenue "K", Brooklyn, NY 11210, (718) 377-4945

WHAT:	CHILDREN'S BOOK WRITING & ILLUSTRATION WORKSHOPS
WHEN:	Annually in autumn, winter, spring and summer
WHERE:	New York, NY
INFO:	460 E. 79th Street, New York, NY 10021, (212) 744-3822

WHAT:	CHISHOLM TRAIL WRITERS' WORKSHOP
WHEN:	Annually in June
WHERE:	Fort Worth, TX
INFO:	Texas Christian University, Box 32927, Office of Extended Education, Fort Worth, TX 76129, (817) 921-7134

WHAT: EMORY SUMMER WRITING INSTITUTE
WHEN: Summers
WHERE: Atlanta, GA
INFO: Emory University, Summer School, 300 White Hall, Atlanta, GA 30322, (404) 727-0675

WHAT: PAUL GILLETTE'S WRITING WORKSHOP
WHEN: Monthly
WHERE: Los Angeles, CA
INFO: 6515 Sunset Blvd., Suite 3008, Los Angeles, CA 90028 (213) 461-9437

WHAT: HARVARD SUMMER WRITING PROGRAM
WHEN: Summers (June - August)
WHERE: Cambridge, MA
INFO: Harvard University, Div. of Continuing Education, Dept. One, 20 Garden St., Cambridge, MA 02138, (617) 495-2921

WHAT: INTERNATIONAL BLACK WRITERS CONFERENCE
WHEN: Annually in June
WHERE: Charlotte, NC
INFO: Box 1030, Chicago, IL 60690, (312) 924-3818

WHAT: IOWA SUMMER WRITING PROGRAM
WHEN: Summers
WHERE: Iowa City, IA
INFO: 116 International Center, Iowa City, IA 52242, (319) 335-2534

WHAT: MIDLAND WRITERS' CONFERENCE
WHEN: Annually in June
WHERE: Midland, MI
INFO: Grace A. Dow Memorial Library, 1710 W. St. Andrews, Midland, MI 48640, (517) 835-7157

WHAT: NAPA VALLEY WRITERS' CONFERENCE - POETRY & FICTION SECTIONS
WHEN: Annually in July and August
WHERE: Napa, CA
INFO: Napa Valley College, Napa, CA 94558, (707) 253-3070

WHAT: NATIONAL WRITERS' CLUB CONFERENCE AND WORKSHOPS
WHEN: Annually in July
WHERE: Denver, CO
INFO: The National Writers Club (NWC), 1450 S. Havana, Suite 620, Aurora, CO 80012, (303) 751-7844

WHAT: NATIONAL WRITERS' CONFERENCE IN CHILDREN'S LITERATURE
WHEN: Annually in early August
WHERE: Los Angeles, CA
INFO: Society of Children's Book Writers, Box 296, Mar Vista Sta., Los Angeles, CA 90066, (818) 347-2849

WHAT: NEW YORK STATE WRITERS' INSTITUTE OF THE STATE UNIVERSITY OF NEW YORK
WHEN: Year-round; write for dates
WHERE: Write for info
INFO: State University of New York at Albany, 1400 Washington Ave., Albany, NY 12222, (518) 442-5620

WHAT: NWC ANNUAL SUMMER CONFERENCE
WHEN: Annually in July
WHERE: Denver, CO
INFO: The National Writers Club, 1450 S. Havana, Suite 620, Aurora, CO 80012, (303) 751-7844

WHAT: OZARK CREATIVE WRITERS INC. ANNUAL CONFERENCE
WHEN: Annually in October
WHERE: Eureka Springs, AR
INFO: Box 391, Eureka Springs, AR 72632, (501) 663-9471

WHAT: PACIFIC NORTHWEST WRITERS CONFERENCE
WHEN: Last Thurs, Friday & Saturday of July, annually
WHERE: Seattle, WA
INFO: 17345 Sylvester Road SW, Seattle, WA 98166

WHAT: PORT TOWNSEND WRITERS' CONFERENCE
WHEN: Annually in July
WHERE: Port Townsend, WA
INFO: Centrum Foundation, Box 1158, Fort Worden State Park, Port Townsend, WA 98368, (206) 385-3102

WHAT: ANNUAL WRITERS CONFERENCE
WHEN: Annually in September
WHERE: Richardson, TX
INFO: Center for Continuing Education, The University of Texas at Dallas, Continuing Education Div., Box 830688, Richardson, TX 75083-0688, (214) 690-2207

WHAT: SHENANDOAH VALLEY WRITERS' GUILD CONFERENCE
WHEN: Annually in May
WHERE: Middletown, VA
INFO: Div. of Lord Fairfax Community College, Box 47, Middletown, VA 22645

WHAT: SKYLINE WRITER'S CONFERENCE
WHEN: Anually in August
WHERE: North Royalton, OH
INFO: Skyline Writers' Club of North Royalton, Ohio, 11770 Maple Ridge Drive, North Royalton, OH 44133, (216) 237-6985

WHAT: SOUTHWEST WRITERS WORKSHOP
WHEN: Annually in September; classes held twice monthly
WHERE: Albuquerque, NM
INFO: Box 14632, Albuquerque, NM 87191

WHAT: STONECOAST WRITERS' CONFERENCE
WHEN: First two weeks in August
WHERE: Gorham, ME
INFO: University of Southern Maine, Portland, ME 04103, (207) 780-4291

WHAT: SUFFOLK LONG ISLAND WRITERS CONFERENCE
WHEN: Annually in April
WHERE: Selden, NY
INFO: 194 Soundview Drive, Rocky Point, NY 11778

WHAT: FESTIVAL OF POETRY
WHEN: Annually, first week in August
WHERE: Franconia, NH
INFO: The Robert Frost Place, Franconia, NH 03580, (603) 823-5510

WHAT: INTERNATIONAL TECHNICAL COMMUNICATION
             CONFERENCE
WHEN: Annually in May
WHERE: Varies, get info
INFO: Society for Technical Communication, STC Headquarters, (202) 737-0035, (703) 522-4114

WHAT: HIGHLAND SUMMER CONFERENCE
WHEN: Annually in June
WHERE: Radford, VA
INFO: Box 5917, Radford University, Radford, VA 24142, (703) 831-5366

WHAT: THE UNIVERSITY OF KENTUCKY WOMEN WRITERS
             CONFERENCE
WHEN: Annually in April
WHERE: Lexington, KY
INFO: 101 Frazee Hally, Lexington, KY 40506, (606) 257-3295

WHAT: VASSAR SUMMER INSTITUTE OF PUBLISHING & WRITING
WHEN: Annually in June
WHERE: Poughkeepsie, NY
INFO: Vassar College, Box 300, Poughkeepsie, NY 12601, (914) 452-7000, ext. 2960

WHAT: WILLAMETTE WRITER'S CONFERENCE
WHEN: Write for info
WHERE: Portland, OR
INFO: Box 2485, Portland, OR 97208, (503) 452-1592

WHAT: WRITING WORKSHOPS
WHEN: Year-round
WHERE: Sacramento, CA and Davis, CA
INFO: University of California, University Extension, Davis, CA 95616

NOTES

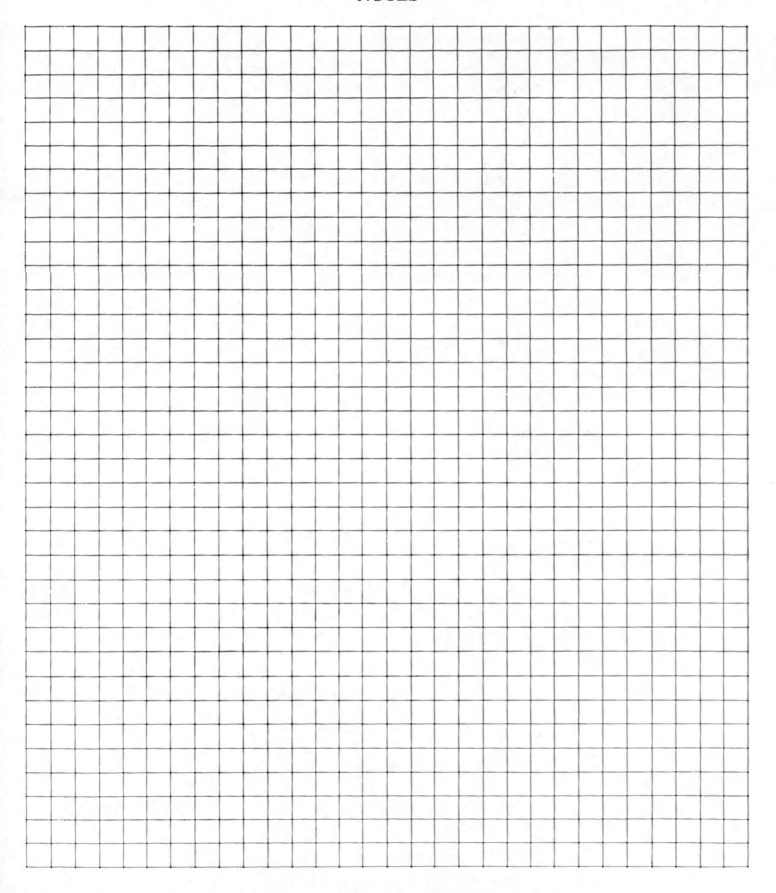

NOTES

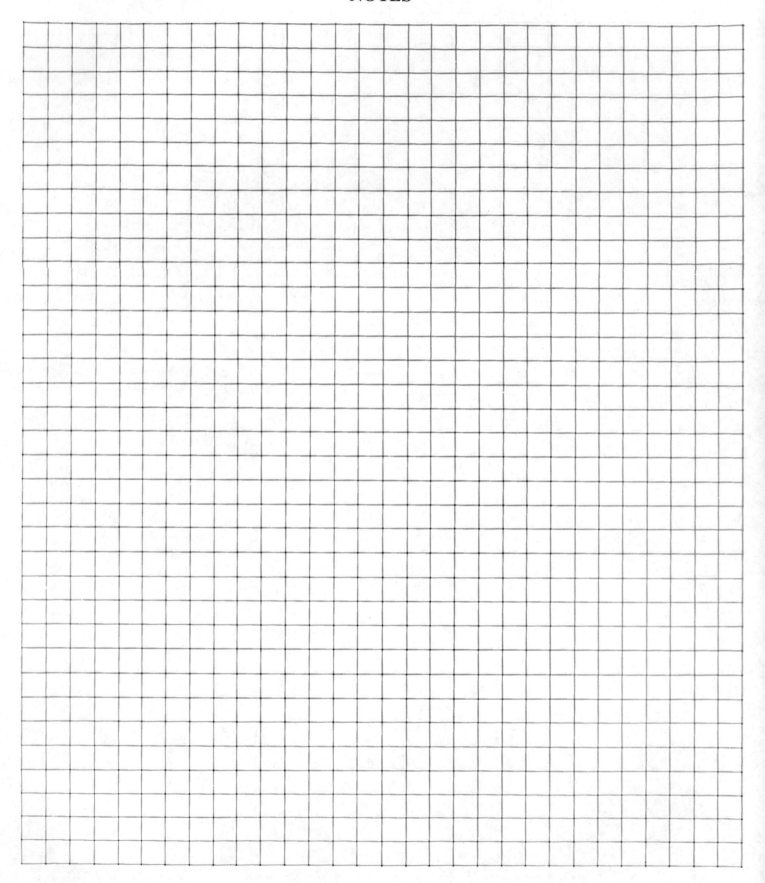

NOTES

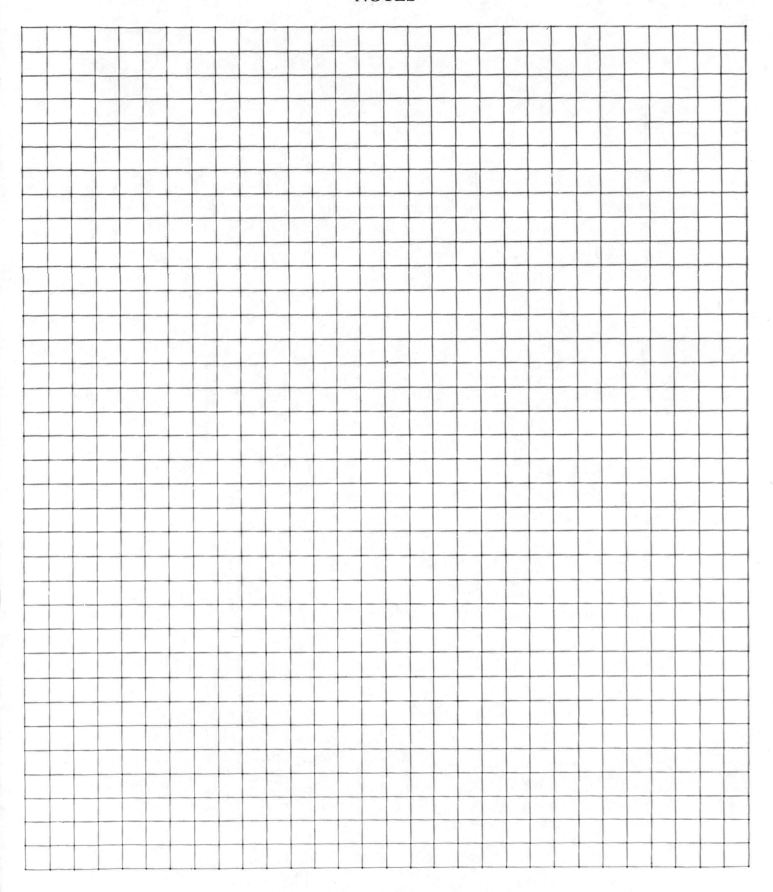

NOTES

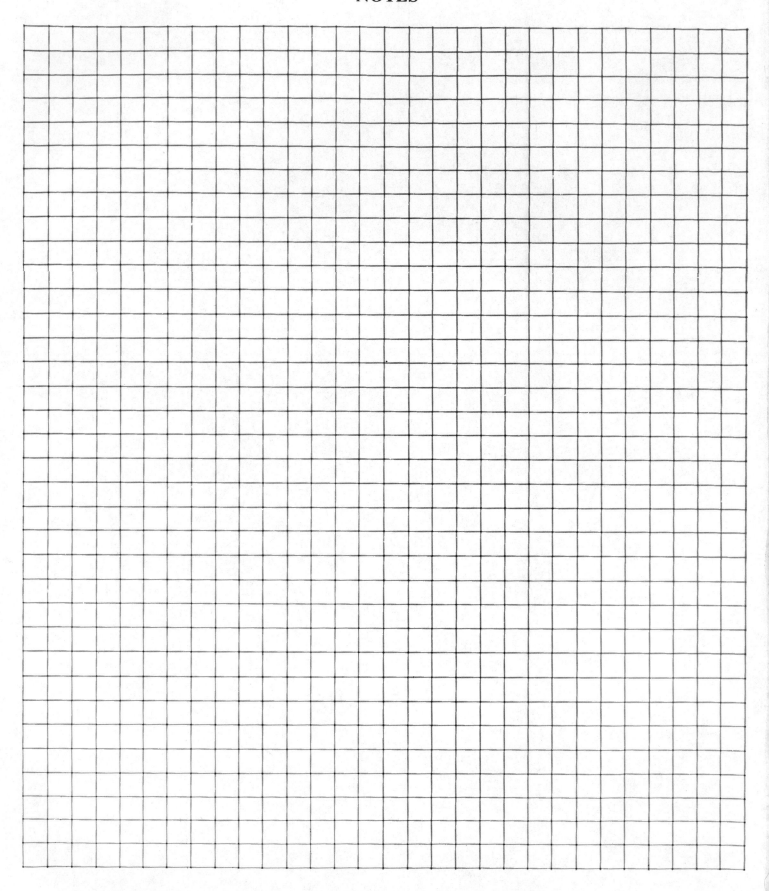